Huntington Library Publications

THE NEWHALL RANCH

The Story of

The Newhall Land & Farming

Company

by RUTH WALDO NEWHALL

THE HUNTINGTON LIBRARY

SAN MARINO, CALIFORNIA

1958

PRINTED BY ANDERSON, RITCHIE & SIMON : LOS ANGELES

DESIGN BY HANS WEHRLI AND JOSEPH SIMON

Contents

Illustrations

Preface

"To the fifth generation!" *With this toast to the great-great-grandchildren of Henry Mayo Newhall, the story of the Newhall Ranch was born. It was at the San Francisco home of Mr. and Mrs. Atholl McBean that thirty members of the Newhall family had gathered for a festive Christmas lunch in 1955. Mr. McBean, Chairman of the Board of The Newhall Land and Farming Company, offered his toast to fifteen young people, ranging in age from three to seventeen. It was with these children in mind that he suggested to me after lunch that I write a history of our company. I think both of us felt that only through such a book would the descendants of Henry Mayo Newhall appreciate the traditions and properties of which they are the heirs.*

In dedication to the fifth generation, therefore, I began my research, but it soon became apparent that the story was more than the history of a family and company. It represented a capsule of California's development and included such elements as the gold rush, early San Francisco business, the rise and decline of the Spanish-Californians, the growth of railroads, and the development of the cattle industry and agriculture.

In writing a ranch history, it is tempting to inject imagination and thus heighten the color, but the writer decided to leave fiction to others. All conversations and quotations appearing in this account were reported by the participants. For material on the life of Henry Mayo Newhall I owe a debt of gratitude to H. H. Bancroft, who, after Newhall's death, asked the latter's wife, sons, and business associates to gather biographical material. These original manuscripts were put at my disposal at the Bancroft Library of the University of California. The Henry E. Huntington Library supplied an excellent manuscript account of the discovery of gold on what was later to be Newhall land, written by Francisca López de Belderraín, granddaughter of the discoverer, Francisco López. The officers of The Newhall Land and Farming Company made available the primary sources—original land grants, legal documents, and complete minutes of directors' meetings.

The compilation of this history would have been impossible without the patient assistance of many people. To Mr. McBean, Mr. Edwin W. Newhall, Jr., and Mr. George Bushell I owe great thanks, not only for their help in assembling material, but for their careful reading and rereading of the manuscript. Miss Margaret Asmus, Mr. McBean's secretary, donated invaluable information, advice, and time. I should especially like to acknowledge the contributions of Mr. William Rand; Mrs. Lucretia del Valle Grady; Mr. Lawrence W. Harris; my husband Scott Newhall; the librarians at the Henry E. Huntington Library, the Bancroft Library, the Society of California Pioneers, and the California State Library; the Southern Pacific Company; and the San Francisco Chronicle.

Through the kind co-operation of the members of the Board of Trustees of the Henry E. Huntington Library and Art Gallery the publication of this manuscript by the Huntington Library was made possible. It was rewarding and touching to know that the late Robert Glass Cleland, whose books furnished me with so much general historical background, read the manuscript just before his death in the fall of 1957. The advice of Mr. John E. Pomfret, Director of the Huntington Library, was especially appreciated; and I should particularly like to acknowledge the conscientious and skillful editing of Mrs. Eleanor T. Harris of Huntington Library Publications.

Finally, as an outsider who entered the Newhall family by marriage, I offer my personal thanks to Henry Mayo Newhall for having left us something more than a material legacy. The bond that he created holds together to this day a large family of diverse character and interests, individuals who still identify themselves with the family unit. It has been a privilege to know each of the more than eighty family members, and to discover how deep are their roots in the soil of California.

R. W. N.

SAN FRANCISCO, CALIFORNIA
JANUARY 1958

THE NEWHALL RANCH

I . . . *The $300 Man*

A CROWD had gathered on the Stockton wharf for the unloading of a steamer from San Francisco. The center of attention, however, was a young man standing on a box, waving a frock coat high above his head.

"Five—do I hear six? Six, six, going at six!" he called with professional ease.

Henry Mayo Newhall was selling off his wardrobe. He emptied his trunk of trousers, shirts, boots, and stockings, but carefully laid aside a pair of gray satin-finished trousers. The trousers he was wearing were the shabby survivors of several fruitless weeks in the gold fields of Douglas Flat.

Many of the people on the wharf were returning, like Newhall, discouraged and empty-handed from the mines. But others had "made their pile" and were eager to exchange gold for fine clothes. Presently the trunk was empty, and Henry counted his returns. He had made $300. This was considerably less than the money he had invested in his futile trip to California, but he regarded it hopefully as a new stake. He went to the ticket window and bought steamer passage to San Francisco for $16.

While waiting for the steamer to leave, Henry watched the crew unload freight onto dray wagons. On one side he noticed four boxes that had split open and had been laid aside because their contents, an assortment of dry goods, were spilling out. He found the consignee of the broken boxes and bought them with the balance of his cash. In the fall of 1850 dry goods were never shipped from the inland port of Stockton to San Francisco; all the traffic moved in the other direction. Henry, however, had plans.

The following day Henry and his broken cases traveled down the San Joaquin River to the long north arm of San Francisco Bay. San Francisco, spreading over the hills at the edge of the bay, had mushroomed in two years from a quiet village of 800 to a bustling city of 20,000. The adobe and wooden shanties that only a year before had crowded the center of the town were now replaced with more substantial brick and even iron houses. Yet, as Carl Meyer described, "Here and there were scattered dilapidated tents, broken down carts and wagons. Boards and parts of half-burned houses lay about everywhere"—evidences of the ravages of the June 14 fire. But amid the ashes business continued active and prepared for the future with fireproof structures and fire engines.

The population of San Francisco seemed even less permanent than its buildings. About ninety per cent of the people were men between twenty and thirty years old, and two-thirds of the population were American. A hodgepodge of Europeans, Mexicans, South Americans, and Australians made up the rest. The waterfront was choked with the hulls and masts of some five hundred ships whose crews had deserted for the gold diggings. Sleeping accommodations, when available, were usually bare board shelves in bunkhouses. Winter rains, cascading down the hills, made such a morass of the streets that it was jokingly reported that several loaded wagons and teams had sunk without a trace at muddy corners. Delays in communication with outside markets often resulted in whimsical situations. For example, carpet tacks, which were used to fasten muslin partitions inside dwellings, at one time sold for $20 a box. When a ship finally arrived with a cargo of tacks, the market was so quickly glutted that tons of tacks were dumped into the streets to give some firmness to the mud. A cargo of iron stoves was also used to pave

4

the streets, and served well until jokers removed the stove lids, resulting in a constant peril for pedestrians.

After the steamer docked at San Francisco, Newhall jostled his way through the freight and luggage and hawkers on the pier and stopped before a sign reading "John Collins, Auctioneer." He proposed to Collins that he borrow the use of the auction block to sell off the contents of his broken boxes, and promised the house twenty-five per cent of the proceeds. The sale brought a handsome profit. Newhall headed directly for a steamship office and bought a steerage ticket to the East Coast for $125. He wanted to go home to his bride in Tennessee, but he was determined not to return impoverished.

He had several days to await the sailing of his steamer, and he spent his first afternoon strolling around the town. On Jackson Street, just off the waterfront, he paused in the doorway of Hall & Martin, Auctioneers. Inside, a lackluster auctioneer was calling his wares to a nearly empty house. Out in front, smoking a pipe, was a young man with the unmistakable air of a proprietor. Newhall approached him.

"Do you need an auctioneer?"

Almer Hall looked in some amazement at the figure before him. Newhall's pointed miner's hat was several sizes too large and came down over his eyebrows. He wore a blue flannel shirt, a wide black patent-leather belt, and satin-finished trousers tucked into miner's boots.

"We do need one," Hall said cautiously.

"What will you pay?"

"We want to pay $300 a month," Hall said. "We've had enough of the $250 kind."

Newhall pulled off his hat, threw it on the ground, and shouted, "I can sell more goods and for bigger money than any man on the stands in California!"

"Well," Hall grinned, "we'll give you a show."

That evening the fog rolled in and it was cold and blustery. When Hall appeared at the auction room about eight o'clock, business was at a standstill. He saw his young friend of the afternoon leaning against the wall. The auctioneer on the stand happily stepped down when Hall beckoned, and Newhall took his place.

"In thirty minutes," Hall reported later, "Newhall had the store densely crowded and two engine companies were there to put out the fire."

By eleven o'clock the goods were almost sold out, and Hall informed his new auctioneer that he was, indeed, a $300 man. When he extended him the privilege of sleeping on the counter, Newhall brought out his steerage ticket, saying he would stay on the job until his steamer sailed.

"Get back on the counter and sell it," Hall said. "The firm will stand the loss."

Newhall sold his $125 ticket for $87.50. Thereafter the company advertised "HALL & MARTIN, H. M. Newhall, Auctioneer."

II...*Saugus to San Francisco*

ENRY NEWHALL'S appearance on an auction block in San Francisco in 1850 was the climax to a life of travel that had begun twelve years earlier when he was thirteen. This wanderlust was out of keeping with the habits of two hundred years of ancestors. In 1630 two Newhall brothers had emigrated from England and settled on the edge of the wilderness at Lynn, Massachusetts, north of Boston. For seven generations Henry's forebears had moved no farther than from Lynn to Saugus, four miles away. Some of the Newhalls had fought in the Revolution. The burial grounds of both towns still hold ranks of weathered headstones carved with the family name.

Henry was born in Saugus on May 13, 1825. Saugus was the location of the first heavy industry in the United States. In 1640 energetic colonists put the Saugus River to work by building an ironworks, driven by giant water wheels, and for a generation the works furnished colonial blacksmiths with plates and ingots. The industry, however, had long been abandoned, and in Henry's day Saugus was a quiet rural town where nearly every citizen combined the trades of making shoes in winter and farming in summer.

Henry's father Jonathan was a member of the Massachusetts legislature. Both he and his wife, Hannah Oatman Newhall, were

7

devout Methodists—Jonathan being a steward of the church—and Henry was named after the local minister. The nine Newhall children, of whom Henry was the fifth, were sent to the Old Rock Schoolhouse, which also served as the Methodist church and social center of the town. When the children had finished their elementary schooling, they were put to work at the bench and in the field. This life of patient labor irked the boy who had within him the thirst for success.

When he was thirteen he left home to sign on at Boston as cabin boy on a ship bound for the Philippines and East Indies. Somewhere in the Pacific trade-winds belt, Henry climbed up the rigging and fell, breaking both legs. The captain was angry; a cabin boy with two broken legs was another mouth to feed. He announced that the boy would be left ashore in Manila, but young Henry was a talker, and he used all his powers of persuasion on the captain. By the time he returned to Boston, Henry had had enough of life at sea, and went home to Saugus. He settled down for one winter at the cobbler's bench until his legs healed and strengthened.

One of his uncles had gone to Philadelphia, which seemed to Henry to be conveniently remote from the family fields. In the spring of 1840, when he had just passed his fifteenth birthday, he announced that he was leaving home again. He had a little money as his share of the family's winter work, but it was only enough to carry him to New York. Joining a surveyors' gang that was laying out a route for a railroad from New York to Philadelphia, he carried the chain to a point just outside Philadelphia and arrived in the city with his earnings in his pocket.

He first accepted employment as a grocer's boy, but a fascination with the wholesale district, where goods were sold at auction, impelled him to apply to Meyers, Cleghorn & Co. on High Street for a job in their auction house. John Meyers, the senior partner, hired him on a sultry August day and put him to work carrying woolen goods from bins to auction block and back again. Within an hour perspiration and the lint from the wool had turned him completely black. He worked for twelve hours—10 a.m. to 10 p.m.—and Meyers remarked, "We've seen the last of that boy!" But the next morning he was back on the job in clean clothes.

A week later he was made an apprentice, to learn the art of auctioneering.

Henry Newhall was with Meyers, Cleghorn & Co. for three years. As his voice changed and deepened, he was allowed to call from the auction block, and he developed a persuasive set of vocal cords. He was eighteen when a member of a firm in Mobile, Alabama, offered him an interest in their company. He accepted and moved to Mobile. Later, when the partnership was awarded to his employer's son rather than to himself, Newhall moved on, first to Pulaski, Georgia, and then to Nashville, Tennessee. He achieved his ambition to own his own business when he joined with another young man to form the firm of Newhall & Baker in Nashville. The partners bought goods wholesale and auctioned them off to retail merchants. Business was good.

In Clarksville, near Nashville, lived the William Whites, Irish Presbyterians, and their three daughters and son. Henry soon formed an attachment to their oldest daughter Sarah Ann, who was twenty years old when they were married in October 1849. The Clarksville *Jeffersonian* noted the wedding with rhymed pun:

> To her Father's hall she bids adieu;
> Her heart is wedded to a Hall that's New!
> May the New-hall's fire be ever bright,
> And heart's affection's shrine be White!

Henry and Sarah Ann had been married only a few weeks when the bride was left alone with her family. It was to be a long time before she bid adieu to her father's hall. Henry, married or not, was still on the move.

This time it was gold in California. Henry sold his interest in the auction business for $8,000 and contributed to the pooled resources of a group of Tennesseeans who were on their way to El Dorado. Kissing his bride good-by, he promised to return with a fortune, and headed for New Orleans.

He chose what was normally the quickest way to California—to Panama by ship, across the Isthmus by canoe up the Chagres River, and by muleback over the jungle trail to Panama City. The Pacific Mail Steamship Company had recently inaugurated regular steamer service from Panama to San Francisco, but the

Newhall party had not anticipated the gold-rush traffic. Not only were ships overloaded, but hundreds of vessels had been immobilized in San Francisco Bay as their crews deserted for the gold fields. By the time Henry Newhall's name came up on the long waiting list for the northward passage, he had become violently ill with fever. Weak and miserable, he lay helpless in the oppressive tropical heat while his partners went on ahead.

Six months later, on June 17, 1850, he finally boarded the Pacific Mail steamer "Panama." He was one of the many young men among the 286 passengers who went aboard with blanket roll and food to live on deck. The "Panama," after stops at Acapulco and San Diego, finally steamed into the Golden Gate on July 6. An enormous crowd was on hand to greet her, eagerly awaiting the seventy-two sacks of mail and newspapers—their first news of the outside world in five weeks. The San Francisco newspapers immediately put out extras announcing that the most important news borne by the "Panama" was that Congress had not yet granted statehood to California.

Newhall, like most gold seekers, did not tarry in San Francisco. He immediately bought a steamer ticket for Stockton, where, according to information left by his party, he could get transportation to Douglas Flat in the Sierra foothills. He put his trunk in storage at Stockton, and continued by stage to the diggings. Eight years later Douglas Flat was to go down in California records as the site of a half-million-dollar gold strike, but in 1850 Henry and his friends found no indication of these riches. At his arrival, there was little left of the group's original capital. Only a few weeks later he found himself out of funds.

This was the low point of Henry Mayo Newhall's fortunes. Returning to San Francisco with the broken boxes he had bought at Stockton, he became the auctioneer at Hall & Martin and cast his lot with the new city of San Francisco.

III . . . *Entrepreneur*

IN THE BEDLAM of San Francisco the auction business was the foundation of trade. As ships arrived auctioneers bought whole cargoes and sold them off, item by item. Auction rooms served as department stores, wholesale outlets, and warehouses, where food, clothing, hardware, and luxury items were sold indiscriminately. The situation was ideal for Henry Newhall, who at twenty-five had already spent ten years in the auction business.

The partners for whom he went to work, Almer Ives Hall and Henry Martin, had been neighbors in Wallingford, Connecticut, and were both twenty years old when they heard the news of gold in California. They arrived at San Francisco on the steamer "Panama" on October 27, 1849, and headed for Sonora. Finding gold dust scarce, they left the mountains for the pueblo of San Jose, fifty miles south of San Francisco. The scarcity of lodgings determined the two youths to enter the hotel business. It did not take them long to find that mattresses, linen, and other hotel supplies were grabbed by San Francisco buyers and never got past the boom-town merchants. Deciding that merchandising would be more profitable, Hall and Martin abandoned their business and went north to San Francisco. They had promised their families that they would be home in two years. With a year and a half left in which to make their fortunes, they started buying merchandise, in a small way, from incoming ships, and selling the goods—shoes, shirts, and sugar—to the highest bidders in the crowded, undersupplied port.

Henry Newhall was an able auctioneer, and the firm of Hall & Martin did well in the spring of 1851. Newhall had not only ability but stamina, and worked ten hours at a stretch calling through a catalogue of fifteen hundred to two thousand items. Then in May their building was burned to the ground in the fifth of the great fires to destroy the jerry-built city. As the smoke cleared away, the partners were offered a more desirable site at the corner of Sansome and Commercial streets, at the foot of Long Wharf. Henry Martin thought that the monthly rental of $350 for the lot, plus the cost of setting up a building on the burned-out site, was too much. Moreover, he wanted to return to Connecticut, the two-year leave granted by his family having almost expired. His offer to sell his share of the business to Henry Newhall was promptly accepted. Six days later, in a still roofless building, the newly located Hall, Martin & Company held its first sale of a few new items and an assortment of merchandise canvassed from friends and neighbors. Proceeds from the sale yielded enough to put them back on a cash basis.

The firm flourished for four weeks, during which time the building was finally completed, when another great fire again put the company out of business. This time Almer Hall decided that he had had enough. As the third building began to rise, Almer Hall sailed for the East, and H. M. Newhall became sole proprietor of Hall, Martin & Company. In the following year the firm name was changed to H. M. Newhall & Co.

With Hall acting as his agent, Newhall was soon placing orders with eastern merchants and buying whole shiploads of merchandise. Henry Gregory, who had crossed the plains with an ox team in 1849, was hired as a clerk and became Newhall's right-hand man. San Francisco was brawling and lusty. One of its major imports was a shipment of enormous gold-framed mirrors for the gaming halls, which were located only a block away from Newhall's auction house. Newhall bought and auctioned shiploads of liquor for the thriving local trade.

Next door to Newhall's auction house was a dark narrow room that served as the dwelling and workshop of an eccentric by the name of James Lick. In 1847 Lick had arrived in San Francisco from South America and had proceeded to buy up the sand dunes and mudholes that were already being converted into a downtown metropolis. Living like a pauper, he aroused suspicion by rummaging in the garbage of hotels and eating places for bones, which he used to fertilize the trees that he imported to plant in San Francisco and San Jose. Later generations were to remember James Lick as San Francisco's greatest educational philanthropist. (His public gifts totaled over $1,750,000.)

Henry did not participate in the gay life of the town, and saved his money to buy a lot in the fashionable South Park district on Rincon Hill overlooking the bay. (Today the Beale Street site of his home has been excavated into a parking lot under the approaches to the James Lick Freeway.) He erected a two-story brick house with a wide veranda across the front and a widow's walk on top in the New England tradition. It was time, then, to fetch his bride. He put Henry Gregory in charge of the business and embarked for Panama in March 1852. In the eighteen months since he had left the gold fields, penniless, he had become a man of substance and property.

At this time Sarah Ann, weary of waiting, bravely packed her trunk and sailed for California. Miraculously, their paths crossed, not at sea, but on the Isthmus of Panama. Persuading her to retrace her steps eastward, Henry went to Saugus to visit his parents, and then to New York to cement relationships with merchants who had goods for export to California.

The long return voyage completed, Sarah Ann moved into the new house in the fall of 1852. Furniture had been shipped from New York, and the big house was pleasant and comfortable. Women were generally unenthusiastic about San Francisco at this time, but Sarah Ann apparently found her position as mistress of a wealthy household preferable to life in a small Tennessee town. She invited the rest of her family to share her comforts. Early in 1853 the Whites arrived with their two younger daughters to live with the Newhalls. They came in time to welcome their first grandchild, Henry Gregory Newhall, born March 4 and named for the man who had just been made a partner in the business.

Newhall's business continued to flourish. Although only in his early thirties, he was becoming a rich man. In the mid-fifties Gilbert Palache, a young man born in Jamaica, joined the Newhall company. In 1857 he married Margery White, the next younger sister of Sarah Ann, and later became a lifelong partner and guiding hand in the business.

In addition to six adults and the servants in the Newhall house, a second son, William Mayo, was born nineteen months after the first, and Edwin White, another nineteen months later. The birth of the fourth child of Henry and Sarah Ann Newhall was disastrous. Both Sarah Ann, then twenty-nine, and her newborn son died. Henry was now the father of three motherless boys, aged five, three, and not quite two. The parents of his deceased wife continued to live in the big house, and their youngest daughter Margaret Jane took charge of the children.

A year later Margaret became the second Mrs. Henry Mayo Newhall. Newhall and his sister-in-law were married by the Reverend William Anderson Scott, an old friend of the White family who had also officiated at the wedding of the Palaches. Dr. Scott was a strong-minded man who was to play an important part in the life of Henry Newhall.

Despite his staunch Methodist upbringing, Newhall had never joined a church. The Whites, on the other hand, maintained the strong Presbyterianism which both sets of their parents had brought from northern Ireland. They had attended Dr. Scott's Presbyterian church in Clarksville and had followed his progress as he built up a large parish in New Orleans. In San Francisco they joined with a group of other local Presbyterians in inviting Dr. Scott to be pastor of the new Calvary Church.

Being a man of firm opinions, Dr. Scott spoke from his pulpit in opposition to the lynch-law methods of the Vigilantes in 1856, and as a result he was hanged in effigy. The church's board of trustees, headed by Newhall, refused to accept his proffered resignation. In 1861 Dr. Scott found himself in deeper trouble. The Civil War was beginning, and the California Presbytery, meeting in San Francisco, was considering a resolution urging ministers to "exhort their people to stand by the Federal Government."

Dr. Scott had lived in the South all his life and had owned a slave for each of his nine children.

"You have no authority from the Bible, nor from the standards of the Church," he said, "to say that Jefferson Davis is a traitor any more than George Washington was." The newspapers abbreviated the quotation to read: "Jefferson Davis is no more a traitor than George Washington was."

The Presbytery meeting had taken place on Wednesday. The next Sunday a mob gathered in front of Calvary Church, and as Dr. Scott walked into the church the crowd hooted and jeered and again hanged him in effigy across the street, labeling the dummy "Dr. Scott the Reverend Traitor." The air was charged with violence, and a patrol of mounted police held the crowd in check.

Henry Mayo Newhall found himself in a strange situation. He was not, by declaration, a member of the church, yet he was president of the board of trustees. He was a strong Union sympathizer, and had contributed heavily to the cause of the North. It was he, however, who climbed out of a sickbed to speak to the congregation in Dr. Scott's defense. Despite long training at the auction block, his public speeches were rare, as he was acutely conscious of the brevity of his formal education. He tried to persuade the church members that politics and religion were separate, but he was unsuccessful. On October 30 Dr. Scott's resignation was accepted. Late that night, under cover of darkness, Newhall brought carriages to take the minister and his family to the wharf, whence they sailed the next day for Europe.

Eight years later, when the passions of war had cooled, the Newhall family was among forty members that seceded from Calvary Church and sought to establish a new church for Dr. Scott, who returned to San Francisco at the end of 1869. The following February Dr. Scott wrote happily to his wife that $45,000 had been raised to buy St. James' Episcopal Church, thereafter called St. John's Presbyterian Church. The deed to the church property was in the name of H. M. Newhall, who had donated a large part of the funds. Although he never joined the church, Newhall remained chairman of the board of trustees until his death.

In 1861 Margaret Jane Newhall presented Henry with another son, Walter Scott, whose middle name was given in honor of the fiery minister. Two years later she bore the last of his five sons, George Almer, who received his middle name in honor of Henry's old friend and partner, Almer Ives Hall. The family was complete.

IV... *Rails in the Sixties*

HE DEVELOPMENT of San Francisco from an overgrown camp to a full-fledged city was rapid. The frequent fires had done their job of cleaning out the shacks and tents. In 1854, only five years after the beginning of the gold rush, solid buildings had spread over the hills, and in size Montgomery Block bowed to few buildings in the world. There were many churches, schools, and civic organizations. Several of the downtown streets had been planked or paved, and debates raged in the meetings of the board of supervisors on whether additional paving should be done by private or public investment. Twenty-one foreign nations had established consulates in San Francisco by 1854. Books and accounts of the "good old days" of '49 were being published. Concerts, theatricals, grand balls, and circuses were the order of the day. The papers, with pride in the city's culture, were glorious in praise and merciless in criticism. In 1856 the *Bulletin* announced a "Grand Full-Dress Concert" of Miss Isabel Land at the American Theatre, adding, "It is presumed that 'full-dress' in California means that the ladies shall not be merely half-dressed, as is sometimes the case elsewhere." In its review the following day the paper represented the concert as "pretty much of a humbug." Another item of news in the same paper reported the prospect of a duel "between two of the parties who had a difficulty in Merchant Street yesterday."

In this gaudy city the business of H. M. Newhall & Co. expanded. There was a transition from auctioneer to wholesaler, and the company branched into insurance. Henry Newhall's profits were large, and he invested in land. The lower part of the city was getting crowded and commercial, so he bought a half block on Van Ness Avenue at the corner of Sutter, and built a more comfortable house for his wife, five sons, and parents-in-law. It was a large three-story structure with a mansard roof and basement quarters for the servants. The bay windows on three sides of the house were surmounted with gingerbread decorations. The drawing room was decorated with rosewood furniture, a square piano, and marble statues (swathed in sheets except on festive occasions).

In 1857 Newhall violated a lifelong precept when he cosigned a note of $90,000 for a friend. He was humiliated when the note came due and the friend was unable to pay. In return for the $90,000, Newhall received from his friend a one-third interest in a worthless property called the San Francisco and San Jose Railroad Company.

Means of transportation were sorely needed in California. San Francisco was still weeks away from the rest of the civilized world by any mode of travel. Nearby towns could be reached only by dusty or muddy roads through ranches, where stagecoach drivers had to stop to open and close cattle gates. A railroad was essential. An overland route out of San Francisco which would avoid both San Francisco Bay and the high barrier of the Sierras often had been discussed. South through San Jose and then eastward through the Mojave Desert seemed a logical route for a railroad.

Beginning in 1850 several abortive attempts had been made to build the first link from San Francisco to San Jose in this transcontinental chain. At that time travelers made the fifty-mile trip from San Francisco to San Jose in six hours by boat or a more leisurely eight hours by stage, at a cost of $32 each way. Operating with private capital, without franchises, and lacking organization, the company in which H. M. Newhall had acquired a one-third interest collapsed in June 1860. A week after the company's demise the *Alta California*, San Francisco's leading newspaper, editorially urged the public to attend a meeting to consider plans for forming a new company.

The second San Francisco and San Jose Railroad Company was organized with a stated capital of $2,000,000, and a number of local businessmen were subscribers to its stock. Only $238,000 was pledged, of which $100,000, or one-twentieth of the funds required, was actually paid. The balance of the $2,000,000 was to be raised by assessments as construction proceeded.

Newhall's $90,000 stock in the earlier road was a total loss, which increased his determination to prove that, properly handled, the railroad could be built. He invested $2,000 in the stock of the enterprise and was made a member of the board of directors. The first business of the board was to take steps to secure the backing of public funds. For ten months not a shovel of earth was turned, but diligent spadework was carried on by conferences with county boards of supervisors. Then in April 1861 the voters of San Francisco, San Mateo, and Santa Clara counties approved the purchase of railroad stock for a total sum of $600,000.

With public money and franchises thus secured, H. M. Newhall started organizing. He saw a likely colleague in Peter Donahue, who had founded in 1849 the successful Union Iron Works, San Francisco's first heavy industry, and later the San Francisco Gas Lighting Company. Donahue was particularly valuable, not only for his experience with public utilities, but because he knew how to procure iron. The Civil War had just started, and the problem of inducing foundries and shippers on the East Coast to deliver materials around the Horn to San Francisco was a trying one. In May 1861 Judge Timothy Dame, a well-known public figure, was elected president of the company; Newhall, vice-president; and Donahue, treasurer.

By September 1863 tracks were laid as far as the Seventeen Mile House near Belmont. This progress called for the first of many gala openings. On September 15 the *Alta California* reported:

Everything passed off pleasantly, the engine succeeded in passing all the native mustangs and wild untamed cattle that with emulative folly attempted a race, and altogether the experiment may be chronicled as a perfect success. . . . An open car carried the excursionists leisurely out to Belmont, stopping occasionally to ward cows from the track with a whistle and to open tollgates, which seem to have been established along the road at irregular intervals—probably for protection of private interests.

At the Seventeen Mile House the celebrations included plentiful refreshments for invited guests of the company, with many bottles for the proper toasts and unlimited oratory.

The following January, just three and a half years after the company had been formed, the "grand opening" of the tracks all the way to San Jose saw San Francisco and state dignitaries and a clamoring mob traveling to San Jose in every available piece of rolling stock, including freight and cattle cars. Some five thousand celebrants were entertained by military bands, a parade of the National Guard, a thirteen-gun salute, and extensive speeches.

By the end of the year, despite a heavy travel load, trouble appeared. The boards of supervisors of San Mateo and Santa Clara counties claimed that money was being spent for salaries and new equipment rather than being paid out as dividends, and they demanded what they claimed were their rights of representation on the board of directors of the railroad company. The company ignored their demands, and the counties appointed an investigator.

Judge Dame retired and his position as a director was offered to Charles B. Polhemus. Polhemus had arrived from South America during the gold rush, and almost immediately had made a fortune as a commission merchant. In 1856 he bought a large part of the Las Pulgas Rancho on the peninsula south of San Francisco, where he built a home and laid out a town which he christened San Mateo. He was a partner of Peter Donahue's in several enterprises, and the tracks and depot in San Mateo had been established on his property. Polhemus, Newhall, and Donahue, deciding that it would be a fatal error to allow the railroad to fall into the hands of politicians, personally bought all the stock held by the counties, and Newhall became president of the company. Traffic continued to increase.

In January of 1865 Newhall signed a contract ordering the first heavy locomotive to be built in California. The order was given to Donahue's Union Iron Works, and delivery was to be made in August. The locomotive's maiden trip to Palo Alto, then known as Twin Trees Station, established a speed record west of the Rockies. Coming through the Bernal Heights into San Francisco, the new engine, called the "California," hit a speed of sixty-seven miles per hour. The passengers, somewhat shaken, were relieved to step to solid ground at the end of the trip.

In 1867 Polhemus sold his shares in the railroad to Charles Mayne. Newhall, Donahue, and Mayne now undertook to consummate their dream of an iron-horse empire and formed a second company—the Santa Clara and Pajaro Valley Railroad Company —to extend the line south to Gilroy. In April 1869 the thirty-mile extension into Gilroy was complete, and the public was again invited to a celebration. According to the *Alta*, "Tables were set with cold turkey, chicken, ham, mutton, cakes, and pies, which received ample attention from the hungry crowd, for they had breakfasted at eight and were pretty sharp set. Claret and champagne were also furnished in liberal quantities." One of the speakers was H. M. Newhall. The *Alta* reported:

Mr. Newhall spoke of the difficulties attending the building of the first section of the road, and many of his friends said he had a wild elephant on his hands in having such a road to manage. He begged to call the attention of those croakers to the fact that he had got the "wild elephant" perfectly tame and in very good order, and that he proposed going on with the railroad business, of which he now had a good knowledge, and would build section after section, with proper encouragement, until Kansas was reached, then St. Louis, and ultimately to New York. The remarks of Mr. Newhall were much applauded.

The next step toward the ultimate goal of New York was taken January 1870 when the California Southern Railroad Company was incorporated to extend the rails south from Gilroy "45 miles to a point in or near Salinas City." William Ralston, president of the Bank of California, entrepreneur of the Comstock, and builder of the Palace Hotel, became an officer in the company.

The California Southern Railroad Company never laid a tie. The previous May the Central Pacific had completed the first

transcontinental railroad by hammering the golden spike at Prom-
ontory Point at the edge of the Great Salt Lake. The Big Four of
the Central Pacific—Stanford, Crocker, Huntington, and Hopkins
—offered to consolidate their interests with those of Newhall-
Donahue-Mayne and to establish a new company to be called the
Southern Pacific Railroad Company. Their plan was to extend
the line south to San Diego and then east to the Mississippi River.
Confronted with the sad example of one small railroad between
Oakland and Sacramento, which had refused to sell out to the
Central Pacific and had been frozen out of business when the Big
Four built parallel tracks, Newhall, Donahue, and Mayne rea-
soned that the offer was attractive. They had invested about
$500,000 each in the railroad from San Francisco to Gilroy; they
sold out for a reported $1,250,000 each. Newhall, Donahue,
Mayne, and Ralston eventually became directors of the Southern
Pacific Railroad Company.

During the early seventies Newhall and Ralston incorporated
another vast project—a railroad which would run the length of
the San Joaquin Valley and across the Mojave Desert to the Colorado River. This was the beginning of a new transcontinental
route. Again the Southern Pacific Company stepped in and
bought their franchises before any construction was commenced.

Thus ended, successfully, Henry Newhall's "railroad era." He
had devoted a decade in San Francisco to auctioneering and
another ten years to railroads. He was now ready for a new
interest, and he had plenty of money to finance it.

V... *The Open Ranges*

HE *californios* belonged to a different world from that of the gold-rush cities of Sacramento, Stockton, Sonora, and San Francisco. The Spaniards and Mexicans who had colonized California in the three-quarters of a century preceding the discovery of gold had their own culture, which continued to exist independently, especially on the ranches in the south, some twenty years after California became a state in 1850. The roots of that culture lay in the assignment of all newly discovered land to the king of Spain as his personal property. California land that had thus become royal domain was distributed in four different categories—missions, presidios, pueblos, and private grants.

The largest grants, many of them in excess of one hundred thousand acres, were for missions. The Franciscan Fathers, led by Father Junípero Serra in 1768, undertook to Christianize and civilize the Indians, to instruct them in catechism, and to train them in farming and animal husbandry. The grants that established the missions were temporary and provided that, whenever the Indian converts had been sufficiently trained, land and livestock would be divided among them for their private holdings.

The presidios were army stations located at San Diego, Santa Barbara, Monterey, and San Francisco. They were built to defend the new land against foreign attack and piracy and in-

23

cluded adjoining grazing lands to maintain the necessary livestock to mount and feed the garrison.

Pueblos, the grants set aside to establish towns and to encourage colonization, were sparsely settled by small merchants, farmers, and the families of army men. (Los Angeles and San Jose were founded as pueblos.) Free plots of land were given to colonists for their homes and orchards; others were set aside for church, town plaza, town hall, and communal grazing lands.

Private grants were large tracts of land bestowed by the king on favored subjects. Actually they were granted by the local governor, as the king's representative. Only about twenty private grants were made in California in the forty years prior to Mexican independence, as this country was unknown and remote.

By 1821 the fever of independence had aroused Latin America, Mexico became independent of Spain, and California was made a department of the new Mexican Republic. The California governor was informed from Mexico City that the old Spanish system of private grants would be continued and that he could grant up to eleven square leagues (48,712 acres) to Mexican citizens who applied for land.

The grant system really became important after 1834, when the wide mission lands, which encompassed nearly all the good grazing lands known to the Mexicans, were taken back from the church and declared public domain. The Mexican government proclaimed that half of the land and cattle of each mission would be distributed among the resident Indians, and the rest would revert to public ownership to be granted to settlers. The heads of the mission organization in California had with great clarity and conviction presented their arguments against secularization, chief among which was the point that the Indians were not ready to take over the management of their own affairs. But pressure from the Mexican inhabitants, who wanted the mission lands for themselves, was too great. The president of the church organization instructed the padres to surrender the mission lands peacefully, and to give up four hundred thousand cattle, sixty thousand horses, and three hundred thousand sheep and swine. In the resulting land-grab the rights of resident Indians were ignored.

The army officers and noncoms, who were sent out to inspect

Henry Mayo Newhall was about 30 when he was photographed with his first wife, Sarah Ann (right) and her sister Margaret Jane. Margaret Jane became his second wife after Sarah Ann's death in 1858.

the mission lands and claim them for the government, looked eagerly at the vast acres, and many filed applications for California ranchos for themselves and their families. Each application was accompanied by a rough map showing boundaries and landmarks. A local official was required to certify to the governor that the land was not otherwise occupied. The applicant had to agree to build a house within a year, to stock his land with cattle, and to live on the property. In theory the grant was to be approved by the departmental assembly, a formality that was not regarded as essential. Surveyors were rare in California during the Spanish or Mexican regimes. Lands were described by hilltops, valleys, streams, large trees, or colored rocks. Boundaries were approximate, being measured by two men on horseback who alternated riding one in front of the other stretching a riata between them.

The *californios* settled in the country of the Coast Range, a narrow belt seldom more than fifty miles wide, extending up the California coast. The Coast Range rises, in most of California's thousand-mile length, directly from the Pacific. It is composed sometimes of rolling hills and often steep and rugged mountains, with grassy slopes cut by brushy canyons and spotted with trees, which thicken to deep forests toward the north. In the extreme south, vegetation is sparse, and behind the mountains lie the great deserts. North of Los Angeles the Tehachapi Mountains connect the Coast Range with the awesome Sierras that form California's eastern barrier. Between the Sierras on the east and the Coast Range on the west is the bowl known as the Central Valley, five hundred miles long and nearly one hundred miles wide, which is the heart of today's California agriculture. Mexican culture was not concerned with the Central Valley nor the mountains to the east, as men and cattle did not live beyond the coastal hills.

The typical ranch house was U-shaped and had adobe walls, earthen floors, and a thatched roof on wooden beams. It was sparsely furnished, and the family lived, to a large extent, on the veranda surrounding the tree-planted central court. Around the house were huts occupied by Indians who rode the range, tended the gardens, and did all the housework for the family. The rancheros were prolific people—a normal family consisted of from eight to fifteen children—and the family group was usually augmented by relatives and visitors enjoying the rancho's hospitality.

Life for the *californio* was not strenuous. The women had servants, and the men spent their lives on horseback. They lived in the kind of feudal agrarian society that was until very recently so prevalent in Latin America, and which in many ways was comparable to plantation life in the South before the Civil War. The leisurely existence of the landholders was underwritten by the slave labor of the Indians. Once or twice a year women and children would climb into heavy oxcarts and, with the men on horseback beside them, would travel for days to attend a wedding, ball, or feast day of bullfighting and horse racing. These occasions called for fine clothing. Men as well as women wore velvets, silks, and gold lace, the only possessions involving the use of money.

Trade was carried on by a barter system, and it has been said that one of the major weaknesses of the colonial culture was the *californio*'s lack of understanding of the use of money. Cash was something to be exchanged for luxuries; necessities were supplied by the land. Before the gold rush money for luxuries came from the sale of hides. The New England sea captains bought California leather for Massachusetts cobblers or for trade in the Spice Islands. Up and down the coast their boats would travel through the surf to load hides, and so heavy was the trade that cattle hides were generally referred to as "California bank notes."

The culture of the *californio* rested solidly on cattle. The "California native stock," as the cattle were referred to, were descendants of an Andalusian breed. In 1769 the "San Carlos," the first ship to bring colonists to California, landed six or seven head of cattle in San Diego. These, and later imported cattle of the same breed, were so well suited to the country that thirty years later there were nearly a million head of cattle in California. The animals were black, often with mottled bellies and lighter stripes along the spine, and had unusually white horns. They were small, light-bodied, and agile. A fat "black steer" weighed from 600 to 800 pounds compared with 1,100 to 1,300 pounds for today's heavy beef breeds.

The routine of the ranches was settled. Once each year, on

every ranch, was rodeo time, when the weanlings were rounded up from the ranges where they had been calved, and were brought into corrals to be branded. Rancheros notified their neighbors of roundup dates, and each ranchero posted men along his borders to see that none of his calves was rounded up with his neighbor's. There were no fences, and cattle grazed freely between ranches. A calf belonged to the owner of its mother's brand; motherless calves became the property of the ranchero on whose land they were found.

At slaughtering time the hides were removed, the fat was tossed into big kettles to be rendered into tallow, and the meat was cut into strips or torn off in sheets and dried in the sun. *Charqui* (jerked beef) was the staple diet of the *californio*. Even so, there was more meat than could possibly be consumed, and it was often tossed aside. A range steer sold for about $4.00 and netted its owners approximately $2.50. Cattle reproduced freely, and the ten acres of grazing land, the average per animal, had cost nothing.

The decline of this pastoral economy began in 1848, when California and the Southwest border states were ceded to the United States by the treaty of Guadalupe Hidalgo. The coming of Americans and traders of many nationalities not only supplied new goods, even to the pueblos and the hills, but also for a time brought unheard-of prosperity to the rancheros. The Americans arrived first as a trickle of colonists in covered wagons, then, in 1849, as a flood of gold seekers. This overwhelming new population needed meat, and steers sold in San Francisco for as much as $75 a head. Buyers from the north appeared on the great ranchos and offered fantastic prices for the black cattle. *Vaqueros* trailed the animals northward up the hilly coast, or over the Tehachapi Mountains and through the marshy San Joaquin Valley. Herds of two to three thousand cattle, in long lines or uneasy groups, plodded fifteen miles a day across deserts, rivers, and mountains to reach San Francisco.

Word of the livestock boom spread through the West as word of gold had spread through the world. Thousands of cattle and sheep came from as far away as Missouri and Texas. Within six years the price of cattle had fallen to $16 a head, and by 1860 there were ten times as many head of cattle as people in California. The boom was over.

This was sad news for the rancheros. They had spent their money, while they had it, in royally extravagant ways. In 1861 the market for beef had vanished. New immigrants, like the sharp German, Henry Miller, had established great beef ranches in the vicinity of San Francisco, and there were plenty of cattle near the city. The rancheros found themselves back in the hide-and-tallow business.

To make matters worse, Nature seemed to be warring against them. Disastrous floods in the winter of 1861-1862 destroyed most of the orchards and vineyards and drowned thousands of animals. A smallpox epidemic swept through the ranchos, attacking master and servant alike. These misfortunes were followed by two years of the worst drought in California history. By the spring of 1863 the range lands lay scorched and barren. With thousands of cattle dying, the rancheros sought to save themselves from total loss by selling their starving herds. The market was soon glutted. The price for cattle fell to $2.50 in 1864, and in the fall of that year some five thousand cattle were sold in Santa Barbara for thirty-seven cents each.

At this time nearly all the rancheros were heavily burdened with legal fees necessary to prove title to their land. They also faced a new phenomenon which they had not suffered under Mexican rule—land taxes. They needed money, a commodity that was easy to get in return for a mortgage. There were few banks in the southern coastal country, but traders and merchants would willingly lend money at compound-interest rates varying from one to four per cent a month. During the boom years many families had made a practice of borrowing money in the spring and paying it back after selling their cattle in the summer, but when recession and drought ruined the cattle business, interest piled up. One ranchero allowed his $3,500 mortgage to go unpaid for eight years at three per cent a month. When the lender finally foreclosed, the ranchero owed $59,000. Mortgage foreclosures and tax-delinquency sales ended the regime of the *californio*. By 1875 the open ranges and their black cattle were owned by the Yankee invaders.

VI...*Grants for a Yankee*

WHEN HENRY MAYO NEWHALL emerged from his railroad activity with well over a million dollars in capital, he looked around for investments. He had bought parcels of real estate all over San Francisco—business property near the waterfront, residential blocks, and wind-blown sand dunes near the ocean. In 1871 he was offered the Rancho El Piojo in Monterey County.

El Piojo ("The Louse") contained 13,300 acres and lay in a wild stretch of rolling hills about 160 miles south of San Francisco. The ranch had belonged to a man by the name of Joaquín Soto. Soto was dead by the time his claim to the rancho was officially recognized by the United States on April 30, 1866. Mortgaged by his heirs, the land came into the possession of Charles B. Polhemus, Newhall's codirector in his railroad enterprises. Polhemus had sold his San Mateo Ranch to his partner Peter Donahue, his railroad interests to Charles Mayne, and now was liquidating his rural landholdings. Polhemus did not own cattle, and leased El Piojo for grazing to partners by the names of Owens and Collins. When Polhemus offered Newhall the Piojo at a price of $5 an acre, or about $70,000, Newhall seized the opportunity to buy the property as well as the 1,500 to 1,800 head of cattle that belonged to the partners. With the cattle he bought the OC brand with which Newhall cattle thereafter were marked.*

Polhemus had also acquired a ranch adjoining the Piojo to the north. The Rancho San Miguelito had long been known as the habitat of enormous grizzly bears. At one time the González family, owners of the rancho and important citizens of Monterey County, had undertaken the dual task of ridding themselves of the grizzlies and providing entertainment for the people of neighboring ranchos by staging bear-and-bull fights. They trained their horses to be unafraid of bears by locking them in a corral with an Indian, who covered himself with a bearskin and made fearful noises and gestures. On moonlit nights the *vaqueros* of the ranch rode into the mountains on their trained horses to find the quarry. Each man in prearranged order took his turn with a lasso, one roping the head, others tying down the feet. Made helpless by five strong riatas, the bear was pulled into a large rawhide sack and dragged for twenty miles over the trails to the adobe arena in the settlement of San Lucas. The temper of the bear after this treatment was not friendly, and he was ready for battle when he was set free to face the bull. The inhabitants of the Monterey region gathered to cheer the contest of onrushing claws and ripping horns—a contest that both sides usually lost.

The González family lost their rancho to the mortgagees in the sixties. About 1872 Newhall bought the 22,135 acres of the San Miguelito at $7.50 an acre, a high price for the time. The ranch had been leased for sheep, but Newhall replaced the sheep with cattle. Since the ranchos adjoined each other, the entire 35,000 acres were put under one administration and became known as the Piojo. Steers were sold in the summer at $20 to $25 a head. In the first years of operation the cattle were driven to the railhead at Gilroy, a trip of one week to ten days.

In 1875 a 48,000-acre rancho, extending over the rolling hills of San Luis Obispo and Santa Barbara counties and known as El Rancho Suey, was put up at auction in San Francisco. Newhall had no time to visit the ranch—a three-day trip each way.

*When the brand was formally registered with the state, some forty years later, a prior claim to the OC brand was discovered, and the Newhall brand was officially changed to O-C.

He knew only that the Rancho Suey was divided between two counties, that it was unfenced except for a few small hayfields, that it included two river courses (the Santa Maria and the Cuyama), and that the sale included 12,000 sheep. Newhall entered a bid of $100,000. By law, two bids had to be offered to make the sale legal. Newhall presented a second bid of $150,000, and since there were no other offers, El Rancho Suey became his for $3.07 an acre, including sheep. When the sale was completed, he traveled down the coast, looked over the rolling hills, and was highly satisfied with his purchase.

The history of the Suey Ranch was associated with famous *californio* families. In 1829 handsome young Romualdo Pacheco, commandant of the presidio in Santa Barbara, married Ramona Carrillo, described as "a handsome and clever girl, famous for a brilliant smile and uncommon vivacity." A month after the birth of his son Romualdo in 1831, Pacheco was the only man to be killed in an abortive insurrection. The young widow, Ramona Carrillo de Pacheco, married Captain John Wilson, a Scotsman who had moved to California. Captain Wilson treated young Romualdo as his own son and reputedly made him the best educated of the *californios*. (The boy grew up to be a successful businessman, and in 1874 served briefly as governor of California.) El Rancho Suey was granted to Ramona Carrillo de Wilson who, like her contemporaries, eventually lost it to the moneylenders.

In 1876, the second year of his ownership of the Suey, Newhall had cause for regret when the second great drought in a decade killed all but two thousand sheep. Newhall was undaunted, and the following year he stocked the ranch with cattle.

The Suey was only one of Newhall's acquisitions of 1875. An ambitious cattleman by the name of José Manuel Soto informed him that another great southern California rancho was available. In 1849 Soto had come to California from Lima, Peru, and after a fruitless year in the Sonora gold diggings, had been attracted to Salinas, a valley inland from Monterey, where settlers had recently discovered the richness of the soil. Soto, having had the good sense not to spend all his money on the Mother Lode, bought the 4,400-acre Santa Rita Ranch, three miles from the town of Salinas.

After setting aside a square mile for a townsite, which he named New Republic, Soto made the rest of the Santa Rita the first completely fenced ranch in Monterey County. He sold lots in New Republic to settlers, and established a newspaper, primarily for the purpose of advocating the building of a railroad from Salinas to Monterey, twenty-five miles away. He envisioned Monterey as a deepwater port through which the products of the Salinas Valley would be carried to the world.

Meanwhile he extended his influence to other parts of the state. At Santa Margarita, near San Diego, he established a landing and settlement, which according to an account of the 1870's "promises to be a complete success." In addition Soto had extensive cattle and sheep holdings in southern California.

When H. M. Newhall's railroad franchise was extended to Salinas, Soto endeavored to interest him in building seaward to Monterey. Newhall saw more profit in extending his railroad southward, as he felt that San Francisco, not Monterey, should be the shipping point for the region.

The drought of the seventies, which wiped out most southern California cattle, left Soto in financial straits, and he decided to mortgage his Santa Rita land. At that time there remained in his name only 1,200 acres at Santa Rita; the rest had been sold, mortgaged, or deeded to his children. His eldest son Pablo was nineteen and held title to 500 acres of Santa Rita. Pablo deeded the land back to his father, and Soto mortgaged his total of 1,700 acres to H. M. Newhall.

Soto thought his cash shortage was temporary in 1875, and was still full of dreams. On hearing that the extensive Rancho San Francisco was up for sheriff's sale, he arranged for Newhall to buy the ranch, with the condition that, at any time within three years, Soto would have the right to buy a one-fourth interest at the original price. With the drought of the following year José Manuel Soto found himself even deeper in debt, and he was thereafter unable to exercise his option. Newhall became sole owner of the Rancho San Francisco and the 1,700 acres of the Rancho Santa Rita. The town of New Republic withered and died.

About twenty miles south of the Suey Ranch, east of Santa

Maria, was the 30,000-acre Rancho Todos Santos ("All Saints"), which had originally belonged to an English merchant, William E. P. Hartnell. Hartnell had come to Monterey from Lima, Peru, in 1822, and was the first foreigner to become a permanent resident of California. In 1825 he married the daughter of Don José de la Guerra, commandant at Santa Barbara before young Pacheco's appointment, and the largest landholder in Mexican California, with Spanish and Mexican grants comprising some 300,000 acres. Five years after his marriage to Teresa, Hartnell became a naturalized and conscientious Mexican citizen. He was a merchant, trader, schoolteacher, rancher, linguist, and interpreter. In 1839 Governor Juan B. Alvarado appointed him Inspector General of Missions. Hartnell was constant in his efforts to protect the interests of all parties in the mission dispute, and in 1841 the grateful governor issued him a grant to the lands of the Todos Santos.

Hartnell died before his land claim had been verified by the United States. He was survived by his wife Teresa and eleven children. By the time the final deed to the land was issued in 1865, ownership of the ranch was vested in varying proportions among several mortgagees and the twelve Hartnells.

In 1879 Robert Conway, who owned a one-twentieth interest in the Todos Santos and leased the entire ranch for pasturage, sold his cattle to Newhall and threw in his undivided interest in the rancho as part of the sale. The following year the Rancho Todos Santos was subdivided and apportioned to the various owners. Newhall received a 1,500-acre parcel immediately adjoining the 5,500 acres conveyed to the Hartnells. The eleven Hartnell children sold their 5,500 acres to Newhall, granting him the use of the land, but reserving title to it until after the death of Doña Teresa, their mother.

The Todos Santos cattle were later to involve Newhall in a legal wrangle by being named as defendants in the Santa Barbara County courts. A man by the name of Albert Abbey accused eight head of cattle of causing damage to his lands. The cattle, he said, were worth $48 and were responsible for damage to the extent of $50. To satisfy the loss, he asked that the "defendants" be turned over to him and made his property. The accommodating justice of the peace, W. W. Broughton, placed the eight defendants on trial in absentia and awarded Abbey $22.50 damages, $25.60 compensation for feeding the cattle, and $45.50 court costs. In the suit it was stated, "Owners of said defendants unknown."

Henry Newhall recognized five of the cattle as belonging to his herd on the Todos Santos. He interpreted the action as a cattle rustler's trick to legalize an outright theft, and asked Charles Fernald, a respected Santa Barbara lawyer, to protest the decision on the grounds that Abbey had failed to mention "the time and place of taking of said defendants." The Superior Court ordered a reversal of the decision and reprimanded Justice Broughton for having "exceeded his jurisdiction." The "defendants" were released to the custody of their owner. The legal expense incurred by Newhall probably amounted to considerably more than the cattle were worth. But this mild-mannered man had a bulldog tenacity in business affairs. He gave away thousands of dollars, but was determined not to be cheated out of a penny.

In less than a decade H. M. Newhall had acquired some 143,000 acres of California's black cattle land. Thus the railroad baron had become a cattle king. Samuel M. Wilson, Newhall's long-time legal adviser, said later: "I examined the titles for him and on several occasions cautioned him against such large investments in one kind of property. But he had much greater foresight than I had."

VII... *El Rancho San Francisco*

L RANCHO SAN FRANCISCO, thirty miles north of central Los Angeles, and today the headquarters of The Newhall Land and Farming Company, was typical of the large Mexican grants. Its history and that of its several owners illustrate in detail the many complex steps by which the Yankee displaced the *californio*.

The story begins with Antonio del Valle, member of a comfortably wealthy family in the Mexican state of Jalisco and a lieutenant in the army of Spain. In 1819, after two California coastal ranchos had been plundered and burned by pirates, Antonio was ordered north as part of a garrison to protect the king's lands and subjects. He left behind his wife and four children. Six years later, upon the death of his wife, Antonio sent for his family. His eldest daughter María had married and chose to remain in Jalisco, but the three younger children landed in Monterey July 27, 1825. His eldest son Ignacio was seventeen. The army of Spain had become the army of Mexico, and when Don Ignacio was twenty, he was commissioned a lieutenant and joined the staff of Governor Echeandía at San Diego. After Echeandía retired, Ignacio became a member of Governor Juan B. Alvarado's staff at Monterey in 1833.

The following year saw the confiscation of mission lands by the government. Ignacio del Valle was sent out to take over the properties and livestock of three of the missions—San Gabriel, Santa Cruz, and Dolores (in San Francisco). At the Mission San Gabriel he found to his horror that the vast stock of cattle on the lands of the richest mission had been slaughtered. The hillsides and valleys of the mission lands were strewn with the rotting carcasses of nearly one hundred thousand animals, stripped of hides and tallow, and shadowed by circling buzzards. The hides and tallow had been sold to coastal traders. Historians differ as to whether the slaughter was carried out by Indians or by local Mexicans, some of whom were in charge of the administration of the mission lands.

North of the Mission San Gabriel lay the huge expanse of the Mission San Fernando, where the transition had been accomplished without damage. The mission lands extended over more than three hundred thousand acres and included fertile valley land that had yielded good grain crops. Ignacio del Valle's father Don Antonio was appointed *mayordomo* (administrator) of the Mission San Fernando, and served in that post for three years, during which time the rancho system got its start. The mission lands, far from being distributed in small parcels to their Indian tenants, were subdivided into large ranchos. Many of the Indians ended by becoming servants on the land they had once worked as mission neophytes.

The northern territory of the Mission San Fernando consisted of the valley of the Santa Clara River, extending east and west. High mountains separated the eastern limits of the valley from the Mojave Desert, and the towering Tehachapis shut it in on the north. El Camino Real, the road that linked the missions, crossed the hills on the south through San Fernando Pass. Since the days of the first exploration northbound travelers, after crossing the pass, had followed the Santa Clara River down the valley to San Buenaventura on the coast.

Sixty-five years earlier Don Gaspar de Portolá, leader of the first land expedition into California, had camped in this valley. His chronicler, who described it as "a place called Castec," noted five Indian villages and that it was an excellent site for a mission.

The valley until then had served as an outpost of the Mission San Fernando grant.

Antonio del Valle admired the spot, and eagerly climbed on the free-land bandwagon. In 1837 he turned over his job of *mayordomo* to Don Pedro López, whose family had been among the early settlers in the pueblo of Los Angeles. Don Antonio announced his intention of settling down in the valley of the Santa Clara and chose as his second wife Don Pedro's daughter, Jacoba Félix López. He applied to Governor Alvarado for a grant of eleven square leagues (about seventy-five square miles), embracing all of the wide upper part of the valley, known as San Francisquito, and extending down the Santa Clara River for a total length of about eighteen miles.

The only serious objection to his application came from William Hartnell, the conscientious Englishman who had been appointed general overseer of the confiscated mission lands. Although Hartnell's in-laws were California's largest landholders, he was dedicated to the idea that some of the lands should be allocated to the Indians. He had his eye on the Santa Clara Valley, which he believed should be assigned to the Indians of the Mission San Fernando. Moreover, he disliked Antonio del Valle, who was described by an American neighbor as "a dried-up little piece of vanity." Hartnell wrote Governor Alvarado that in ordinary years, according to the San Fernando Indians, the Santa Clara Valley was the only place in the area where there was a certainty of harvesting a crop. He advised against the grant to Don Antonio "for the sake of pleasing one individual who does not at all deserve to be preferred," and said that it would mean "incalculable damage to the whole working community." But Governor Alvarado was apparently friendly to the Del Valles. He pushed Hartnell's objections aside and on January 22, 1839, signed the grant. The description of the land was set forth in the grant:

Bounded on the West by the arroyo Piro, which comes down from the mountains on the North, and runs into the River called Santa Clara, and a line extended across said River at the mouth of said arroyo towards the South to a large Oak Tree (Roble) which is situated on the Southern side of the River upon the top of a hill and standing alone which tree is well known there being no other oak tree but

37

this. On the South by a line drawn from said tree to the East through the hills until it reaches the door (La Puerta) or bar which is in the high road from San Fernando to San Francisco at the very foot of the cuesta of San Fernando where the road is very narrow and where it was formerly completely fenced by bars tied to an Oak Tree (Encina) the mountains coursing down on either side and leaving a very narrow pass. And thence in a straight line along the base of said mountains to the Arroyo Taburga, on the East following said arroyo in a Northerly direction until it empties into the River Santa Clara, and thence Northerly until striking the high hills and for the Northern boundary. Thence following the tops of said high hills along the cliffs nearest to said River Santa Clara, to the Arroyo Piro, the same indenting the Valley between said hills with the boundaries above mentioned.

The Del Valles moved to the rancho with cattle and sheep and built an adobe house at the foot of the hills on the southeastern edge of the broadest part of the valley, where they could look across the river and up Castaic Canyon. They named their domain El Rancho San Francisco.

Jacoba Félix presented Antonio with two children, a boy, José Ignacio, and a girl, Concepción. Don Antonio's retirement to ranch life was brief, for two years after he had taken possession, he died. Ignacio, Antonio's elder son by his first marriage, was then thirty-three, older than his stepmother, and not yet married; the youngest child, Concepción, was an infant.

Spanish-American families were large, and Jacoba Félix had many relatives. She moved to Los Angeles for a while, and some of her relatives came to the ranch. Among them was an uncle, Francisco López, who had recently finished his studies in mining at the University of Mexico. He brought his own cattle to the ranch and rented pasture for them.

López's knowledge of minerals combined with a happy accident to make him the central figure in a historic discovery. One March day in 1842 Don Francisco prepared for his daily ride up the canyons. Attired in sombrero, silk neckerchief, bearskin chaps, and armed with pistol, rifle, and hunting knife, he made a colorful picture as he rode ahead of his Indian servant. The pair stopped for lunch under an oak tree; while the servant spread out the blanket and served the food, Don Francisco dug the onions his wife had asked him to gather. He used his hunting knife to cut into the ground, and as he pulled up an onion he noticed glittering particles around the roots. The first California gold had been discovered.

Don Francisco gave a great shout. Other matters forgotten, he and his servant loaded their saddlebags with earth from the spot and returned to the ranch house. The next day all the men of the family rode to the San Fernando Mission to show Don Francisco's find to his brother Don Pedro. In honor of the occasion special rosaries were said, followed by the singing of hymns and the dancing of quadrilles.

The next day Don Francisco carried his samples to Los Angeles, and a special messenger was sent to Mexico City with the news. The find received little publicity, as compared with James Marshall's discovery on the American River six years later, but local excitement ran high; Indians from the ranchos and townsmen from Los Angeles flocked to the diggings. In November of 1842 the first gold from the Rancho San Francisco was sent to the Philadelphia mint. The yield of that year was between $8,000 and $10,000; the following year, $42,000. As late as 1858 Cyrus Lyons, a local merchant, sold a single nugget for $1,928. For many years small amounts of gold were mined from the canyon, which had been named Placeritos ("Little Placers").*

Two years after Antonio del Valle's death, Jacoba Félix came back from Los Angeles with a new husband, José Salazar, and moved into the ranch house. Life on the rancho—the roundups, the annual selling of hides, the cultivation of food crops by the Indians—went on as usual, complicated only by the discovery of gold. Ignacio had been appointed tax collector and was charged with the burdensome job of watching over the prospectors and collecting taxes on the gold they found. One of Antonio's children by his first marriage died—probably of smallpox, which had reached epidemic proportions.

By the terms of the treaty of Guadalupe Hidalgo of 1848 the

*Lucretia del Valle Grady, granddaughter of Ignacio del Valle and wife of the late Henry Francis Grady, ambassador to Greece and to Iran, wears a bracelet made of gold from the Rancho San Francisco.

Del Valles and Salazars automatically became United States citizens, and their rights to their lands were affirmed. Ignacio del Valle, believing that the Spanish-Californians should make a place for themselves in the new government, went to Monterey as a member of the territorial assembly. In 1850 he was a municipal judge (alcalde) in Los Angeles, where Spanish was still the working language of the courts. He was chosen county recorder in the first election under American statehood and then was sent to the California legislature as a representative of Los Angeles County.

While Ignacio was carrying out his civic responsibilities in Los Angeles, the Rancho San Francisco was the location of another historic occurrence. About New Year's Day, 1850, two weary young men, William Manly and John Rogers, hobbled up to the door of the Del Valles' adobe ranch house. More than two weeks earlier they had left the Bennett-Arcane party, a little band of eleven people, including three women and four children, in an infernal desert to the east. They had walked more than two hundred miles to get help.

Many years later, Manly wrote of their first view of the Rancho San Francisco as they crossed the last ridge of desert:

When the summit was reached a most pleasing sight filled our sick hearts with a most indescribable joy. I shall never have the ability to describe adequately the beauty of the scene as it appeared to us, and so long as I live that landscape will be impressed upon the canvas of my memory as the most cheering in the world. There before us was a beautiful meadow of a thousand acres, green as a thick carpet of grass could make it, and shaded with oaks, wide branching and symmetrical, equal to those of an old English park; while all over the low mountains that bordered it on the south and over the broad acres of luxuriant grass was a herd of cattle numbering many hundreds if not thousands ... such a scene of abundance and rich plenty and comfort bursting thus upon our eyes, which for months had seen only the desolation and sadness of the desert, was like getting a glimpse of Paradise, and tears of joy ran down our faces.

The two men, desperate after days of subsisting on hawks and crows, shot and killed a yearling steer, and used the hide to fashion new moccasins. The following day they came to the

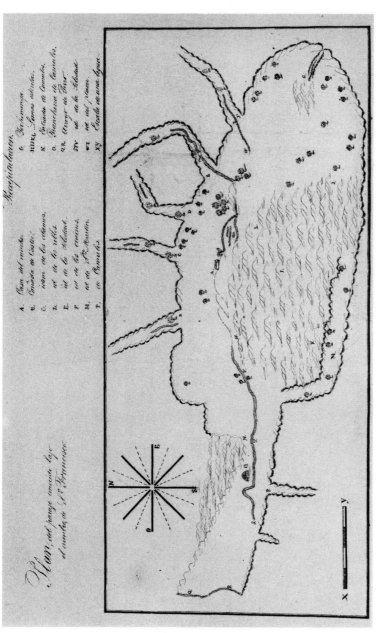

Plan of the Rancho San Francisco, about 1840. Del Valle Collection in the Huntington Library.

Ignacio del Valle (1808-1880). *Pierce Collection in the Huntington Library.*

ranch house, which "was of a different style of architecture from any we had ever seen before." They approached with trepidation, afraid that they would be set upon for having killed the steer. There was a mule tied near the doorway, and when a man of the household finally appeared they indicated that they wanted to buy it, but he shook his head. As they spoke no Spanish, they attempted no explanation of their predicament, but inquired, "San Francisco?" The man pointed northward. A second man appeared and traded a quart sack of corn meal for Rogers' patent-leather belt.

Manly and Rogers turned away and started slowly north, Manly limping as a result of a lame knee. They stopped only a few hundred yards away by the edge of the Santa Clara River to build a fire and bake corn meal and water. When a band of horsemen approached, they hastily buried their cash and readied their guns. However, the group was friendly. One of the horsemen spoke English and they learned to their horror that San Francisco was not just over the hill but five hundred miles away. The man offered to procure horses and to accompany them to Los Angeles.

The next day they rode as far as the Mission San Fernando and a man on the trail told them that they would do better to get horses and supplies at the Rancho San Francisco. They retraced their steps, and, with their bilingual friend to explain their plight, were warmly received. A "dark-skinned woman" on the ranch, whose features reminded Manly of his mother, was particularly solicitous. She arranged sleeping quarters for them in a store-house, and showed them how to grind wheat into flour, which Manly described as "hard, slow work." They breakfasted on tortillas, meat, and baked squash, and the woman instructed them in a vocabulary of simple Spanish words. In sign language she asked how many women and children were in the desert party. The people at the ranch (Manly never learned their names) made up packs of beans, wheat, dried meat, and flour. They equipped two horses with packsaddles and ropes, and showed the two *yanquis* the proper way to pack. Manly and Rogers laid all their money on the table. The rancheros took thirty dollars and pushed the rest back. At the last minute the woman appeared with four oranges, indicating with gestures that they were for the children of the party.

The provisions saved the lives of the Bennett-Arcane party. Three weeks later, as the group turned for a last look at the desert where they had expected to perish, Manly gave it a name, saying, "Good-bye, Death Valley!"*

During these early years of statehood Ignacio did not have to worry about the ranch. Buyers from San Francisco flocked to the Rancho San Francisco to buy beef on the hoof to feed the hungry new population. In three years California had grown from a remote Mexican-Indian community into a fabulously wealthy state with a soaring population. But life was changing. The treaty of Guadalupe Hidalgo had promised to honor Spanish and Mexican land grants. The next step was up to the United States Congress, which meant a five weeks' delay in communication. Congressmen were puzzled by the frequently asked question that nobody could answer: "Is there land in the public domain in California for settlers?" Tales of the rancheros and their holdings had spread eastward. The rancheros protested against squatters and trespassers; new immigrants complained, even more loudly, that "Mexicans" drove them off land that was neither fenced nor used.

Congress set up a land commission to settle the issue, and the commission was given three years, later extended to five, to investigate and approve or disapprove the claims of former Mexican citizens to land grants. The Land Act of 1851, as finally written, made it incumbent on the landowners to prove ownership and worked a great hardship on the rancheros. Either side, government or claimant, had the right to appeal the commission's decision to the courts. When the commission awarded a claim, the government automatically appealed to the courts. In order to retain his land each ranch owner thus was forced at great expense to climb the legal ladder, usually to the United States Supreme Court.

*This account is taken from *Death Valley in '49* by William Lewis Manly. The historical marker at Bennett's Well in Death Valley erroneously reports the name of the ranch as the Rancho San Francisquito.

For the Del Valle family the first order of business was to establish the legal heirs, since Antonio had died without a will. The Los Angeles County Court ruled that his widow, Jacoba Félix López de del Valle de Salazar,* was entitled to one-third of the estate; the other two-thirds went to the four surviving children—Ignacio, Magdalena, José, and Concepción—and to the heirs of the older sister María, who had died in Mexico. The next step was for the two Los Angeles attorneys, Jonathan Scott and Ezra Drown, who had handled many land-grant cases, to file a claim with the land commission on behalf of the Del Valles. The claim to the Rancho San Francisco, filed September 2, 1852, was numbered 318. During the next two years several old friends of the family filed affidavits testifying to the fact that the grant was valid and that the Del Valles had occupied the Rancho San Francisco since 1839.

Ignacio del Valle was deeply attached to the ranch and clung to it stubbornly as his friends and relatives moved away. He took the first step to increase his interest in 1852, when he bought his sister Magdalena's one-sixth share for $4,500, recording the transaction with the county. Two years later his mother, stepfather, brother, and sister Concepción signed another legal document granting Ignacio the right to build and own a home on the ranch.

In that year of 1854 Ignacio was forty-six, and presented a short and sturdy appearance. He had a keen and determined mind and, unlike his father, he was popular both with the Spanish-speaking community and with the new Californians. In the boom years following the gold rush the ranch had been profitable, and he was eager to settle down and use his new capital to develop it. He brought his fifteen-year-old wife Isabel to live at the main ranch house while he began establishing his own estate at the far end of the ranch, some ten miles down-river. The first construction was a four-room house for a foreman, surrounded by huts for Indian laborers. Ignacio supervised the planting of vineyards and orchards of olives, apricots, oranges, and pears. Then he increased his holdings by buying two-thirds of his

*Since U. S. court clerks were apparently unable to cope with this string of Spanish names and Doña Jacoba was illiterate, all records show the grant awarded to Jacoba Félix, which has led some to deduce that the Del Valle ranch was sold to a Jacob Félix.

mother's interest in the ranch, which gave him title to nearly half of the undivided grant.

The day after New Year's, 1855, the land commission awarded the Rancho San Francisco to the Del Valles. The federal district attorney, as was the custom, appealed the award to the United States District Court. Since 815 claims were in process (604 were eventually confirmed and the rest dismissed as fraudulent), the case moved slowly, and another twenty years passed before the final deed to the property was issued. Meanwhile the land commission's decision was accepted, and the Del Valles were free to regard the land as their own.

Ignacio was a happy man. His first child Raimundo had been born; he had acquired a major share in the Rancho San Francisco; cattle prices had been good. He had money, position, and prospects. But bad times came quickly. Although he had acquired a large interest in the land, his only claim was to his house. He had bought the interests of both his sisters and the major part of his stepmother's share, but his brother José and his stepmother had the right to mortgage their interests. Since the ranch was undivided, these mortgages compromised Ignacio's share. When cattle prices fell drastically in 1856, the Del Valle family became entangled in a series of complex financial maneuvers that are typical of what happened to the *californios*.

Acting on the assumption that the depression in cattle prices was temporary, Jacoba Félix and her husband José Salazar began to borrow. Two years later prices had not improved, and the Salazars repaid their first loan by securing a larger one from another lender, William Wolfskill. An ingenious and respected trader, Wolfskill had inaugurated commerce with wagon trains operating between Santa Fe and Los Angeles; he was one of the founders of the wine and fruit industry in California and a leader in all major southern California commercial transactions. His loan of $8,500 to the Salazars gave him a mortgage on the Rancho San Francisco. Ignacio looked on helplessly while the Salazars signed further mortgages on his beloved ranch; one to a pair of Los Angeles merchants and another to the lawyers who had handled their claim and whose $1,000 fee they could not pay. For two years the loans went unpaid with compound interest accumulating at the rate of one and a half per cent a month, a total of forty-two per cent at the end of this period.

In desperation Ignacio went to Wolfskill, the major creditor. He wanted, somehow, to save his portion of the Rancho San Francisco before it was lost to satisfy the mounting interest on his stepmother's debt. Wolfskill agreed to pay off the other creditors and to assume the entire debt of $16,350. He then filed a demand for foreclosure, and the sheriff advertised that the Rancho San Francisco would be sold to satisfy Wolfskill's claim.

The details of the sheriff's sale had been arranged in advance. In the small community of southern California, it was well known that there would be no unexpected bidders. Wolfskill, by agreement, bid the $16,350 owed him, and was awarded the ranch. Then he deeded five-elevenths of the property to Ignacio, including a small parcel belonging to Ignacio's brother José. By this device the Salazars no longer had any interest in the ranch, and Ignacio was free of the burden of their debts. In other respects the property continued to be operated as an undivided unit.

Ignacio hastened to go ahead with the development of his house. He put the Indians to work making clay bricks to build a proper house near the foreman's cottage. He named his residence Camulos, because of the juniper trees which grew only there. The twenty-room home, with wide verandas surrounding a central patio, was finished in 1861. The courtyard was planted with shrubs and fruit trees, and in the corner of the garden a chapel was erected. A small fountain near the chapel watered a flower garden which supplied a daily bouquet for the altar. A vigil light burned continually on the altar, and was never extinguished until the last Del Valle left Camulos in 1924. The family was summoned for daily prayers by the chapel bell, and once a month by special arrangement with the archbishop a priest came to celebrate Mass.

Ignacio's family continued to grow, and about one hundred people—family, servants, and workers—lived at Camulos. The family had taken in eight Los Angeles orphans whom they reared with their own three children. It was a self-contained life; the only food which had to be brought in was sugar and salt. The rancho produced its own meat, vegetables, and fruit; manufactured wines and brandies from its own grapes; and milled its own flour. Fifty people could, and often did, sit down in the great dining hall. For the ladies, who had to travel by oxcart (horses were for men), it was a seven-day trip to Los Angeles. Life was serene, devout, and unhurried. Ignacio had lived at Camulos for two years when the great drought of 1863-1864 withered the trees and killed the cattle. Camulos, like other ranchos, was hard hit.

A new discovery was to save Camulos once again for Ignacio. In 1859 a hole bored in the ground near Titusville, Pennsylvania, had yielded a substance that was a ready substitute for whale oil and coal oil which then furnished illumination for much of the civilized world. It was called petroleum ("oil of rocks"). Professor Benjamin A. Silliman, Jr. of Yale found evidence that California was rich in the same substance. He reported his findings to Colonel Thomas A. Scott, president of the Pennsylvania Railroad, who had acquired major oil interests in Pennsylvania and was seeking to expand. Scott sent his nephew Thomas R. Bard to California to stake claims, and young Bard arrived at the best possible time for land acquisition. The great drought had killed most of the cattle and sheep, and the rancheros were hopelessly in debt. Either directly, or at sheriffs' sales, Bard bought all or most of nine great ranches at a price of one dollar an acre or less.

The most promising oil territory lay in the valley of the Santa Clara, where Indians and mission fathers had for years gathered the sticky black seepages from the hills to use as fuel. The Rancho San Francisco appeared to have the greatest possibilities for oil, and Bard approached Wolfskill and Ignacio del Valle. Their discussions apparently encouraged Ignacio to decide that he would be better off with a few well-cultivated acres and some capital.

On March 18, 1865, the three co-owners of the Rancho San Francisco—Wolfskill, Ignacio, and José del Valle—sat down with Bard and their respective lawyers. Bard paid $53,320 for the entire Rancho San Francisco. Wolfskill received $21,307, José was paid $5,811, and the balance went to Ignacio. Then Bard sold to Ignacio for $500 the 1,300 acres surrounding the Camulos house. From this transaction Ignacio not only retained his home, orchards, outbuildings, and vineyards, but acquired over $25,000 in cash.

Bard, who later became an important figure in the California oil industry and eventually United States Senator from California, was not acquiring the Rancho San Francisco for himself. He promptly deeded it to one of his uncle's companies, the Philadelphia & California Petroleum Company.

Just as drilling was to start, a forgotten child appeared on the legal scene. A local lawyer, searching title records of the Rancho San Francisco, came across the name of María Pimienta. María was the child of Ignacio's long-dead older sister who had remained in Mexico when the rest of the family had emigrated to California. María and her father, as heirs of one of Antonio del Valle's children, arrived to claim a two-fifteenths interest in the ranch. The courts ruled in 1868 that the Pimientas' claim was valid. The search for oil came to a halt while the land was surveyed and a partition arranged. The survey measured Camulos, Ignacio's property, at 1,340 acres. The Pimientas received two parcels totaling 6,460 acres, which they sold a short time later to a San Francisco buyer for fifty cents an acre, and returned to Mexico with only a few hundred dollars each, after lawyers' fees had been paid.

The petroleum company, in the meantime, had protected itself against loss. After selling a few marginal acres to farmers and merchants, the company mortgaged the remainder of the land to a man named Barclay, and secured a loan of $75,000, a sum considerably higher than the cost of the ranch. By 1872 no oil had been discovered. Furthermore the California oil bubble had burst. The need for petroleum was not great, and the market was flooded with good oil from Pennsylvania. Barclay sued for foreclosure in 1872. The Philadelphia & California Petroleum Company had sold part of the adjoining Simi Ranch and the Las Posas Ranch and in the two sales had collected $62,839 which they paid to Barclay. The company still owed $33,000 in principal and interest, and on April 17, 1873, the remaining 40,000 acres of the Rancho San Francisco were put up for auction. The property was sold to Charles Fernald and J. T. Richards of Santa Barbara who gave a note for the $33,000. Six months later, when Fernald and Richards had not made payment, the sheriff ordered another sale. But the sale was postponed when José Manuel Soto, the Peruvian from Salinas who had founded the town of New Republic, heard about the foreclosure. Recognizing a good buy, he told the sheriff he would find a purchaser, and he did.

On January 15, 1875, Henry Mayo Newhall acquired for $90,000 the entire Rancho San Francisco—excluding Ignacio del Valle's Camulos and a few corner pieces that had been sold by the oil company. These small parcels were acquired later as they became available. Included in his original purchase were the 6,460 acres that had been awarded to the Pimientas and that had since passed through several hands.

Ignacio del Valle mortgaged Camulos to Newhall in 1879 for $15,776. The following year Ignacio died, at seventy-two, leaving one-third of Camulos to his wife Isabel, and two-thirds to his six children, with the provision that the property remain undivided until after Isabel's death. Newhall did not take steps to foreclose the mortgage on Camulos. He was too entranced with the remaining 46,460 acres and their magnificent possibilities.

VIII... *Foundation for the Future*

ROM THE BEGINNING of his ownership, the Rancho San Francisco was Newhall's great interest. Possibly one of the attractions was that the Southern Pacific Railroad, building south from San Francisco Bay, was about to cross the ranch to make the first rail connection between the bay area and Los Angeles.

Newhall's early railroad enterprises had launched a coastal route to Los Angeles, a route difficult and devious because of the hills which lay near the ocean, but this railroad was not completed until nearly thirty years after Newhall bought the Rancho San Francisco. The Southern Pacific Company had surveyed another easier route out of Oakland, a short ferry trip across the bay from San Francisco. From Oakland the railroad had to cross one range of hills to the flat Central Valley where tracks could be laid, without grades or tunnels, for over two hundred miles. The rails moved into a short mountain stretch across Tehachapi Pass to the Mojave Desert. From there it was an easy thirty-two-mile run to the head of Soledad Canyon on the Rancho San Francisco.

When Newhall bought the ranch, the tracks were approaching its borders from two directions. Rails were being laid down Soledad Canyon from the north, and to the south hundreds of Chinese laborers were digging the San Fernando tunnel, beyond

49

which were the tracks to Los Angeles. (The bones of Chinese who did not survive the labor were temporarily interred in a cemetery on the ranch and later shipped back to the land of their ancestors.)

Newhall's first move was to build a station and two houses on the open land at the east end of the ranch, where Soledad Canyon joined the valley of the Santa Clara, alongside the right of way which he promptly granted to the Southern Pacific Company. The station was located at the present site of the town of Saugus. This site was not sheltered by the oak trees that covered the rest of the open valley, and violent winds blew down the canyon from the Mojave Desert. Blazing sun alternated with wind-blown sand to make the location a horror. When the railroad came through from the north early in 1876, Newhall decided to move the station three miles to the south in the shelter of the hills. The station was to be the nucleus of a town which Southern Pacific officials voted to name Newhall. That same year the California Star Oil Company, whose Pico Canyon field was coming into production, built California's first refinery alongside the tracks, just outside the townsite.

The land allocated to the town of Newhall was divided into lots, and the vacant land was deeded to the Western Improvement Company, a Southern Pacific subsidiary that served as real estate agent for new towns created by the railroad. Proceeds from the sale of town lots were to be divided half-and-half between Newhall and the company.

Newhall reserved two central square blocks for himself. He envisioned his town as a major southern metropolis. In the name of his ranch superintendent D. W. Fields, he incorporated a hotel company and, on one of the blocks, built a hotel which was described by a historian at the time as "the best in the State outside of San Francisco." Across the street from the hotel Newhall laid out a town square, planted it with young trees, and daily during the hot months sent up a water wagon from the river to irrigate the park. Thus Newhall spent the first winter in town development, commuting back and forth from San Francisco.

Until the completion of the San Fernando tunnel the town of

Newhall was the end of the line from the north, and passengers left the train here to take stages going over the hill to San Fernando. The town soon acquired a store, a livery stable, a lumberyard, and several saloons. For another eleven years passengers going to Santa Barbara and other coastal points got off the train at Newhall and took the stage through the length of the ranch to Ventura.

Newhall liked the ranch life and favored it for his sons. Henry Gregory, the eldest, when a student at Yale, had joined a party organized by a Yale professor during summer vacation to survey unmapped portions of the West. Staying with the expedition until it was too late to return to college, he decided to join his father in the operation of his properties. In the autumn of 1878 ranch work began in earnest when Newhall and his son set up their headquarters in a frame house that had been built to replace the Del Valles' old adobe, destroyed by an earthquake. The Newhall house standing today at the location of the feed yards was built higher on the hill than the Del Valle house. To supply the ranch with water, Newhall dammed a stream and installed one thousand feet of pipe to the house. He built a large horse barn and nearby a strange structure which he claimed as his own invention, a five-sided outhouse, to accommodate a number of ranch hands at one time and thus get them to work in time in the morning.

Newhall began spending more and more time on the Rancho San Francisco. He hired a motley crew of Mexicans, Indians, and Chinese and housed them in tents. A contemporary wrote: "As upon a battlefield, under canvas, his plans were formed, and from under canvas his men sallied forth to execute them. It was a battlefield. He was warring with the powers of Nature." The first year they plowed five hundred acres of open land. Though the crop of wheat and barley was sowed late, the grain averaged over fifteen bushels to the acre, and the total yield was over 280 tons.

Encouraged by the results of the summer harvest, Newhall moved his men down the river to the west end of the ranch, where the winds were not so dry and the weather was more even and humid, and gave them shovels to dig ditches from the river to irrigate the flatlands alongside. There he planted corn, alfalfa, and flax, as well as tropical and subtropical plants such as sugar cane, bamboo, and citrus fruits. Near the station in the town of Newhall the workers planted an experimental orchard of about fifteen hundred assorted fruit trees—apples, pears, walnuts, nectarines, peaches, plums, apricots, and oranges. All flourished but the oranges; the winter climate at the eastern end of the ranch was less mild than that ten miles down the valley.

Cultivation in the second winter and spring was extensive. About three thousand acres—nearly five square miles—were cleared of sage and chaparral, and an additional five thousand acres of open land were broken up. Using six plows, each drawn by a team of horses, the men plowed sixty acres a day to a depth of four and a half inches. Horse-drawn sowers spent two months planting the plowed ground. The rains of 1879-1880 were good, and the July harvest produced a grand total of six thousand tons —twelve million pounds—of wheat.

Later years proved that the bumper crop had been a freak. During the ensuing four or five years hot winds from Antelope Valley struck the wheat just as the heads were filled and tender and before the starch had formed. The fields of ripening grain were reduced to a harvest of parched straw. The spring of 1880, the last good season for wheat, was also the last good season for its grower.

During his late forties and early fifties Newhall was a man of seemingly inexhaustible energies. With one hand he bought and administered ranches; with the other, he lived the life of a busy city executive and family man. Despite his other activities he never neglected his first company, the primary source of his wealth. The firm of H. M. Newhall & Co., successors to Hall & Martin, had matured as an active part of the San Francisco business community. Cargoes arrived not only from the company's East Coast agents but also from Europe and the Orient. Agents operated in many of the world's major cities, buying whiskey from Scotland and hemp from Manila, and selling insurance on high-seas cargoes. Twice a year Newhall himself or other company executives went on buying trips to New York. Newhall continued to mount the auction block from time to time to call through a catalogue. But investment in real estate had held his interest from the start of his career. He bought the old broken-down Tehama House, which had been a hotel for the gold-rush traffic, just before the Bank of California decided the California Street site would be an ideal location for its new building. Another acquisition was a church at the corner of California Street and Dupont (now Grant Avenue), which he turned over to the California Academy of Sciences, of which he was a member. Among the twenty-three parcels of San Francisco property that he owned, several were in the neighborhood of the present Southern Pacific terminal in the area bounded by Mission, Townsend, Third, and Fourth streets. He also owned a group of sand dunes in what is now the residential Richmond district, as well as property in Pacific Heights and lots near his old railroad right of way in the outer Mission district. As the San Jose railroad extended south, Newhall acquired 353 acres in Belmont; a lot, wharf, and building in Redwood City; and land and buildings in San Jose and Gilroy.

In 1874 James Lick, Newhall's eccentric neighbor in the early days, made use of profits from his real estate ventures to set up a trust fund of $700,000 "for the purpose of constructing . . . a powerful telescope, superior to and more powerful than any telescope ever yet made . . . and also a suitable observatory connected therewith." He appointed Newhall one of the seven trustees of the fund. This was the first step which ultimately resulted in the construction of Lick Observatory on Mt. Hamilton, near San Jose. Newhall and his fellow board members did not serve long. The entire group was dismissed when one of the trustees had the temerity to suggest that Lick's illegitimate son be provided with some money by his father. The second board in turn was later replaced by a third.

The summary dismissal of Newhall and his colleagues as trustees of Lick's scientific project did not greatly affect them, for they were preoccupied with other matters. The Bank of California, overexpanded by William Ralston's many ambitious projects, shut its doors, and that same afternoon Ralston drowned while swimming at North Beach. Newhall was among the group of San Franciscans who put up money to help re-establish the bank. He then joined its board of directors.

Despite his time-consuming and active business life, Newhall did not neglect his large family. His five sons received their elementary education in the San Francisco public schools and were sent East to high school. Only the two eldest went to college; Henry's failure to finish Yale was a grievous disappointment to his father. The second son, William Mayo, or Mayo as he was always called, graduated from Yale and took a law degree at Columbia. The other three, despite their father's displeasure, went from high school directly into business.

The big three-story house at Sutter Street and Van Ness Avenue, with its many bedrooms, its parlors, conservatory, and billiard room, was a busy place. The Newhalls lived comfortably, with servants, carriages, and jewels that were the marks of comfort and prosperity, but without the lavish display so common among the wealthy men of the city. The whole family attended St. John's Church on Sundays, and Newhall quietly supported several of the less fortunate members of the congregation.

Newhall was companionable to his sons. Mayo later wrote: "There were seldom, if ever, any of the difficulties or differences between him and his sons that frequently happen between a father and members of his family. He appreciated the fact that as his sons grew older they ceased to be children and became men; and with that view he took them into his confidence in a business as well as a social way."

The father was resolute in his purpose to establish each boy in a career and to encourage him to be financially independent. As each son approached maturity, he was given a job and paid a salary. If a son borrowed money from his father, he gave a note which was repaid with interest. Young Henry devoted himself early to ranch life; the other four sons were trained in H. M. Newhall & Co. William Mayo, on finishing law school, handled the legal work for the company; Edwin and Walter were trained as auctioneers; and George spent his school vacations in the company's offices and warehouses.

Newhall had planned to establish his sons in the business and to retire to his ranches. In 1880, the year of the big wheat crop, he announced that he would no longer be active in H. M. Newhall & Co. His intentions were better than his performance, for when he was in town he could not stay away. In the summer of 1880 he went to Chicago for a meeting of the board of directors of the Southern Pacific Company, which happened to coincide with the annual encampment of the Knights Templar in Chicago's Lakeshore Park. During the encampment he came down with food poisoning and arrived home a sick man. He never again felt completely well.

In the spring of 1881 Newhall spent part of the month of April touring the ranches with Mrs. Newhall and his old friend and partner Almer Ives Hall. Then they hurried home to be present for the arrival of the first grandchild. The child, a boy named Almer Mayo Newhall, was born May 14, 1881, the son of Edwin and Fannie, who was Hall's only daughter. The celebration of his birth was short-lived. Three days later Fannie Hall Newhall died of puerperal fever at the age of twenty-two. Edwin, with his baby son, moved back into the family house.

In early March of the following year Newhall was again at the Rancho San Francisco. While riding around his properties, he was injured when his horse stumbled and fell. He was taken home by train, and on March 13, at the age of fifty-six, he died in San Francisco.

The eulogies written of Henry Mayo Newhall were flowery and abundant. They stressed his integrity, his charity, his love of family, his support of worthy causes, his personal simplicity. Such qualities have been praised in many people—*de mortuis nil nisi bonum*—but the traits which enabled the young boy to break from seven generations of New England tradition and grow to success are those which lie beyond the usual Christian virtues. Newhall was hardworking and extremely aggressive. He had a versatile mind and was an independent thinker; he was an apostle of tolerance—rare qualities in the little-educated. His devotion to duty was well demonstrated by his generous gifts to the church.

The characteristic which made him of interest to later generations was his business sense—his membership in that society of men who seize the opportunity to dominate the forces of their times. Newhall shared the driving qualities of a sizable group of men who rapidly converted California from the pastoral scene of the Spanish-Americans into a metropolitan community. He wanted to build for the future—a drive understandable in a man with five sons—and he had the foresight to judge in which direction the future lay.

The five Newhall sons, ca. 1873

Mayo   Henry   Edwin

Walter   George

Henry Mayo Newhall's first San Francisco home, at 334 Beale Street.

Newhall, California, in 1878, showing hotel and town square, livery stable (upper left) and railroad station (lower right). From History of Los Angeles County (1880).

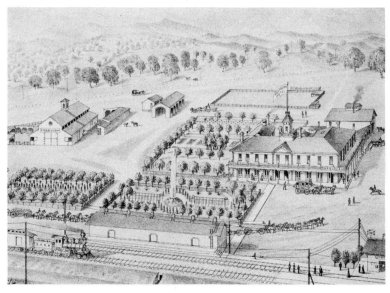

IX ... *A Company of Five*

ENRY MAYO NEWHALL'S carefully accumulated fortune now lay in the hands of his widow and five sons. Drawn two years before his death, Newhall's will expressed some of his hopes and concern: "I will, and earnestly enjoin Executors and especially my wife to see that my children are respectably reared, supported, and maintained, that their morals, health, and education receive the greatest care and attention, and enjoin upon my children to treat and regard my wife with utmost affection and protect and comfort her."

Margaret Jane Newhall, the stern Presbyterian who had raised her sister's three sons and given them two half brothers, was still distressed that her husband had not been a church member. She talked to her sons of his spirituality and godliness and virtue to convince them and, possibly, herself that his place in Heaven had not been jeopardized by his failure to accept confirmation in the church.

Although Margaret may have had troubles of the spirit, she had none in worldly matters. Henry Mayo Newhall bequeathed between $2,500,000 and $3,000,000 to his wife and sons. To Margery Palache, Margaret's sister, and her three children he willed a total sum of $31,000.

Newhall left "homestead, furniture, etc., with all my watches and jewelry, carriages, horses" to his wife, to pass to his sons on her death. To maintain the establishment, the will provided that "executors, out of funds of estate in their hands shall at all times during the life of my wife pay to her and for her own use and to and for such purposes as she may see fit to apply the same, any and all money from time to time as she may require and request of them to pay to her."

The rest of the estate was left, share and share alike, to the five Newhall sons. The executors were enjoined to convert his holdings "without sales of real estate" into cash and, after paying debts and bequests, to use the money for the support of his sons or for the improvement or purchase of real estate. The executors were Mrs. Newhall, her brother-in-law Gilbert Palache, and the two oldest boys, Henry and Mayo. Mrs. Newhall speedily resigned her position, and the three remaining executors decided to revise the provisions of the will by settling stated possessions on Mrs. Newhall, rather than giving her "money from time to time." They concluded, therefore, to assign to her not only her home but the twenty-three parcels of land in San Francisco and the property in San Jose and Gilroy, plus a one-quarter interest in the remainder of the estate.

In addition to the land the estate consisted of about $100,000 in cash, $339,000 in city and county bonds, assorted mining and bank stocks, the business and stock of H. M. Newhall & Co., "a certain lot of diamonds," livestock and buildings on the ranches and in the town of Newhall, and the family plot at Laurel Hill Cemetery where Henry M. Newhall was interred alongside his first wife, her parents, and his daughter-in-law.

After the city properties and stocks and bonds were assigned to Mrs. Newhall, the rest of the estate was administered as three separate enterprises. H. M. Newhall & Co. was appointed as business manager for the entire estate and continued as commission merchants and insurance brokers. Mayo, the legal adviser, and George, recently graduated from high school, worked with their uncle Gilbert Palache in this company.

A second firm, Newhall Sons & Co., was organized to continue the auction business. Edwin and Walter, trained at the auction block by their father, decided to continue in his footsteps. However, the development of communications and commerce soon reduced the auction business to an outlet for used goods, there being little need for auction sales of new merchandise. Newhall Sons & Co. ran heavily into debt and within two years it was dissolved. Edwin and Walter went into other family enterprises.

The other assets of H. M. Newhall, comprising "all the land that is not in cities," were assigned to Henry, the oldest son, who had worked with his father on the ranches. The property included all of the ranches—the San Francisco, the Suey, the Piojo, the Todos Santos, the Santa Rita—and a few acres of land in Belmont and Menlo Park.

Settlement of the estate took a little over a year. On June 1, 1883, the articles of incorporation of The Newhall Land and Farming Company were drawn up under the laws of California, with a stated capital of ten thousand shares at $100 a share. Mrs. Newhall was given twenty-five hundred shares, and the remainder of the stock was divided into five parts of fifteen hundred shares each. By this time the youngest son George had reached his twenty-first birthday and could have his full rights as a stockholder in the corporation. Thus did the 143,000 acres of California ranch land pass to the second generation of Newhalls. Such inheritance often brings difficulties. But there was no quarreling; the brothers were close and their relationship was friendly.

Henry Mayo Newhall had adjusted his style of living to the seven people in his family, and had employed the required number of servants to maintain a proper household. His widow and his unmarried son George, who was to live with his mother for the eighteen remaining years of her life, saw no reason for change. The other sons soon married and established their own households, and all retained the same comfortable way of living. A few months after his father's death Edwin married the girl who had been his wife's roommate at Dana Hall and a maid of honor at his first wedding. Mayo and Henry were married within the next two years. Ten years later each of these three sons had four children; Walter was also married, but had no children. The fortune that had supported a family of seven and their servants in one house had to be extended to care for twenty-two persons in five establishments.

Living in an age when corpulence was a symbol of prosperity, the five brothers presented a massive appearance. Edwin, the heaviest, was slightly over six feet tall. At sixteen he weighed 200 pounds; at twenty-seven he was moving toward 350 pounds, which he reached at forty and maintained the rest of his life.

At the organization meeting of the board of directors of the newly formed company, Henry was elected president and Mayo, the second son, vice-president. Gilbert Palache, who was older and an experienced businessman, was named secretary; H. M. Newhall & Co. was appointed treasurer. The board had jurisdiction over some 220 square miles of California land, which, except for the embryonic town of Newhall and a few hundred acres sown to grain, was undeveloped range land. Following the counsel of H. M. Newhall as defined by his will, the sons organized to retain and develop the property. The company was incorporated for a period of fifty years, which appeared at that time to be a logical term. In fifty years, presumably, their own life spans would be over.

The first item of business to be taken up by the directors of the new company was the matter of trespassers. Squatters had been a problem since the early days of the Mexican grants, and the Newhalls, like other ranch owners, inherited the difficulty along with the land. The Pacific Coast Oil Company became a troublesome violator of boundaries when it acquired title to the West's first refinery at Newhall and laid the first oil pipe line in California across the Rancho San Francisco to the refinery from its Pico Canyon oil field. The two-inch pipe had been laid without lease or easement. Mayo was delegated by the board to meet with Senator Charles M. Felton, president of the oil company, to determine what could be done about the unauthorized pipe lines and the violations of property boundaries.

Senator Felton was an able politician, and Mayo commented after meeting with him that his conversation had abounded in "glittering generalities." The senator promised to look into the matter and to apply for leases sanctioning "the privileges his company enjoyed." When a report came from the superintendent of the Rancho San Francisco that the oil people not only continued to trespass in Potrero Canyon but constantly left cattle gates open, the directors determined to take more drastic action. For a full year Mayo tried to make appointments with Felton, but the senator was always elsewhere. Word came through that he was campaigning for re-election. Finally George Newhall, accompanied by a lawyer, marched over to the oil company's San Francisco office and served legal notice to vacate. Confronted by that legal gun, they surrendered and signed a lease.

More dramatic was the story of another squatter who worried the directors. On the Todos Santos Ranch, formerly owned by Hartnell, lived the Olivera family, consisting of an old man known as José Chiquito and several grown sons. When the land came into the possession of the Newhall company on Mrs. Hartnell's death in 1884, the Oliveras claimed some two thousand of the Newhall's seven thousand acres. People of the region, knowing that the family had often sheltered the notorious bandit Tiburcio Vásquez, regarded the Oliveras as "dangerous desperadoes."

Mayo was directed "to open negotiations looking to the Oliveras' speedy abandonment of their claim." He hired an interpreter, rode in a buckboard from the town of Santa Maria to the Todos Santos, and had a long and friendly conversation with José Chiquito. The old man claimed that he had a grant to the land. When asked where the document was, he waved his hand vaguely eastward and said that someone was keeping it for him. Mayo finally suggested that the matter be settled by the courts and José Chiquito, shaking his hand, agreed to abide by the court's decision. While the matter was pending court action, the Newhall company offered to buy the Oliveras' claim or to build another house to establish them elsewhere. Both offers were refused. When the Oliveras were unable to produce a grant, the court awarded the Todos Santos to The Newhall Land and Farming Company.

José Chiquito kept his word and moved to Los Alamos, a village about twenty miles inland. His sons, however, were not so obliging and remained in their ancestral adobe. Three or four times sheriff's deputies arrived in force and moved the Olivera possessions to the county road. Each time the Oliveras brought them back. "Finally," Mayo Newhall later recounted, "it was decided to make a drastic move and a man was found who, for the consideration of $100, would go on the premises and take possession for us. It was difficult to find a man of enough nerve to do this, as the family had the reputation of being extremely dangerous. One day, when all members of the family were absent from the premises, the house, in some mysterious manner, caught fire, which consumed all the woodwork—the roof, floors, et cetera." The Oliveras left and never returned.

This rough-and-ready solution to the Olivera problem was not typical of the Newhalls' dealings with their Spanish-speaking neighbors. During the same period another group of *californios* were treated quite differently. When Ignacio del Valle died in 1880, leaving Camulos to his wife and six children, the $15,000 mortgage on his property, held by H. M. Newhall, was the estate's only major debt. Three years later the sheriff of Ventura County announced that a sale of Camulos would have to take place to satisfy the mortgage. Doña Isabel del Valle filed a petition asking that she be allowed to sell small parcels of land privately and not be forced to put the family home and its acres on the block.

At this juncture The Newhall Land and Farming Company suggested a solution. The company had an offer for some of its land adjoining Camulos. However, the prospective sale was complicated by the fact that the boundary between Camulos and the rest of the Rancho San Francisco was irregular, following the shifting course of the Santa Clara River. The Newhalls agreed at a directors' meeting that "the land toward the west boundary of the San Francisco Ranch, from its remoteness, was of little use to the Company." They decided that if the Del Valles would survey the border between the Rancho Camulos and the Rancho San Francisco and change the boundary to a straight line, the Newhall company would tear up the mortgage. Judging by rates prevailing at the time, the survey probably cost the Del Valles something less than $100. By straightening the boundary line, they came out with about six hundred additional acres and no mortgage.

X . . . *The Ranch Business*

THE NAME "The Newhall Land and Farming Company" did not properly describe the company's operations in the early years. The company did very little farming—stock raising was the prime interest. The ranches, altogether, carried about six thousand head of cattle, three thousand sheep, and two hundred and fifty horses. Because of their locations, the several ranches were operated as three separate units: the Rancho San Francisco; the Suey and Todos Santos, which were only a few miles apart in Santa Barbara County; and the Piojo and San Miguelito ranches in Monterey County. Each of the three units was under the direction of a resident superintendent.

Operations at the Suey, Todos Santos, and Piojo were handicapped by their distances from railroads. In the eighties and early nineties the terminal point of the coast railroad was at Soledad, about fifty miles south of Gilroy. Newhall had terminated his railroad at Gilroy before it was purchased by the Southern Pacific Company. Soledad was eighty miles from the Piojo and one hundred and fifty miles from the Suey—a long drive for cattle and cow hands. Cows on the Piojo were considered productive for the time, producing an eighty per cent calf crop each year. However, the rainy season was so late on the Piojo that steers were not ready for market until midsummer when beef was abundant and prices were lowest. On the Suey Ranch, to the south, the calf crop was a poor sixty per cent. On that ranch grass came early, and steers could be made ready for the high-priced early spring market. Statistics indicated that the Piojo was more suitable for operation as a breeding ranch for calves and that the Suey was better suited to the growing of beef for the market. The change in operations had to be delayed until after 1895 when the railroad was finally extended through Santa Barbara, and calves could be shipped from one ranch to another. But cattle, at best, returned only a slight profit. The Newhall ranches were too far from San Francisco to warrant shipment there, and other California towns were too small to import much beef.

The most profitable venture on the ranches in the early years was the raising of horses on the Rancho San Francisco, where the animals could be loaded directly on trains. While cattle sold at $20 to $25 a head, horses brought $50 each in San Francisco, where they were used to pull the horsecars that served for public transportation.

Roundups, fence building, and a little dry farming of grain in the spring were the pursuits that filled the ranch days. Most farming was actually done by tenants who rented the land on a share-crop basis. Writing some fifty years later, Mayo Newhall declared that the company had never lost money through a tenant. The lease system had proved so successful and several tenants were so well thought of that they were hired as ranch superintendents.

The first few years of operations under the company were difficult. In 1884 all the hay and grain at the Rancho San Francisco were ruined by late rains and fog. That year the ranch showed a loss of $14,500. With still greater losses the following year, M. P. Nicholson, superintendent of the San Francisco Ranch, was called to task for employing too many ranch hands. Planting was curtailed the following year.

At the end of the second year of company operations the brothers, assembled as directors, took stock of the situation. The ranches had become luxuries, draining money from the family purse, and they agreed that something should be done. Only Henry was primarily interested in the ranches, but he did not have the strong executive temperament needed to run a large absentee organization, a difficult task at best. Mayo proposed giving up his law practice to devote himself to active management of some of the ranch holdings. The directors voted to divide the properties, assigning to Henry the active supervision of the San Francisco and Piojo, and to Mayo the responsibility for operations at the Suey and Todos Santos.

Henry built a comfortable house in Los Angeles and moved there with his bride to be closer to the Rancho San Francisco. During the summer of 1886 he noted the increase in labor rates and the poor return from cattle. He was an engineer by nature and had studied surveying at Yale. It was he who had shared his father's vast development plans for the land.

At a directors' meeting held in October Henry recommended making a detailed survey of the Rancho San Francisco (only its borders had been surveyed), to enable the company to plan irrigation and to locate roads and ditches. He also suggested a water survey which would include estimates on drains, ditches, and reservoirs. The purpose of this, he explained, was to "subdivide the land and attract colonizers and settlers." His object was to price the land and to put it in the hands of real estate agents for subdivision. He recommended the formation of a "Newhall Water Company" which would own all the water rights on the Rancho San Francisco. Stock in the company would be issued in proportion to the land sold. Thus, as the land changed hands, "the water stock is disposed of to landholders who will thereby become the managers and regulate their own affairs."

To have followed all of these suggestions would have involved considerable expense. Pressure was developing. In 1887 the deficit was over $40,000 and the young men, with their growing families, were not financially able to cope with the continuing losses. They were obligated to sell the properties. Some of the parcels of San Francisco real estate, which had accounted for a large part of their father's estate, had been sold by the senior Mrs. Newhall who had then advanced her sons a $50,000 loan to tide them over.

The only feasible part of Henry's plan was to offer the land for sale. A contract to sell the Piojo and San Francisco ranches was executed with two British agents. The company also advertised its ranches "for sale, in whole or in part," in various commercial publications. The brothers priced the Piojo at $700,000, $20 an acre, and put a slightly higher price on the land at the Rancho San Francisco. While a few small parcels were sold to local buyers, the prices were generally too high for the market at the time. Only thirteen years had elapsed since the same land had been acquired at $2 to $5 an acre.

In 1887 the Southern Pacific Company completed its line running the length of the ranch westward to Ventura and connecting the valley route with the coast. The spur track branched off at the point where H. M. Newhall had located his original station. Land for a new townsite was set aside at the junction where the old station site had been abandoned. Henry suggested the name of Saugus, his father's birthplace in Massachusetts, and the name was adopted for the new town.

Henry's days as president of the company ended abruptly in 1889 when he suffered personal financial reverses. He sold some of his company stock to other members of the family, borrowed on the rest, and left for Europe with his wife and three-year-old daughter. He continued to hold the title of president for four years.

Walter, the fourth son of the family, succeeded Henry as manager of the Rancho San Francisco. He moved into Henry's house in Los Angeles where he engaged in a real estate venture with three other young men. The company, which owned a hill in Los Angeles, promoted the sale of lots by establishing a funicular railway designed to carry residents up and down the hill. When the business was liquidated, each partner emerged with a profit of one hundred thousand dollars.

The five years from 1885 to 1890 had established the pattern of living which the sons were to follow for the rest of their lives. Walter and Edwin worked hard to repay the debts incurred in the failure of the short-lived Newhall Sons & Co. Walter's successful Los Angeles real estate transactions provided funds for the repayment of his debts. Edwin at first divided his time between H. M. Newhall & Co. and a Seattle department store, but when the department store showed dwindling profits he settled down into H. M. Newhall & Co. He and his youngest brother George bought the interests in H. M. Newhall & Co. owned by their three brothers and made that business their career.

Mayo, meanwhile, turned his full attention to the farming company and traveled tirelessly between the ranches. In 1894 he was formally elected president. With his university training and degree in law, Mayo was the best-educated of the brothers. He possessed an individual elegance of taste and manner and loved good music and good books. He was slimmer than his brothers and dressed impeccably. Despite these personal characteristics he threw himself into the rough ranch life, attended cattlemen's meetings, investigated feeding and breeding methods, and negotiated horse sales.

In 1896 the directors voted monthly salaries of $400 to Mayo and $300 to Walter as managers of the ranches, thus establishing a salaried-director policy that was to cost the company a considerable sum.

Henry had returned from Europe in 1895 and was appointed engineer and surveyor for the company, a position that was far more to his taste than the tedious details of administration. He surveyed the borders of all the ranches and mapped the irrigable fields on the Suey, Piojo, and San Francisco ranches. After his death in San Francisco in 1903, his wife and three surviving children left the coast and thereafter divided their time between England, the Continent, and New York. Henry's family was the only group that had no further direct connection with ranch administration.

The water company suggested by Henry was never formed. However, in the last months of the nineteenth century The Newhall Land and Farming Company organized its first subsidiary, an oil company. From the time of the first oil exploration in California various companies had held oil leases on the San Francisco Ranch. The directors agreed that, since experts were so sure there was oil underneath the grazing lands, they would do well to participate in the business. As a result The Newhall Oil & Development Company was organized with a stated capital of $500,000. The new subsidiary issued 500,000 shares of $1 par value stock to The Newhall Land and Farming Company in return for title to 5,000 acres of land. The land selected for this oil development was at the western end of the ranch, adjoining the Del Valles' Camulos Ranch. The Newhall Oil & Development Company, whose president was Gilbert Palache, executed several leases but drilling was never started. The modest dividends produced by the new company came entirely from rental payments.

During the last years of the nineteenth century, following the panic of 1893, the nation was in an economic slump; farmers and cattlemen were desperate. The Newhall Land and Farming Company had to decrease its dividends during the years 1891 to 1895, and then stopped paying altogether.

The directors, at a board meeting held on July 5, 1900, voted again to sell the Rancho San Francisco. Walter, manager of the ranch, was selected to negotiate the sale of all 45,000 acres for $750,000, about $17 an acre. At the following meeting of the directors he announced that he had found two partners, Messrs. Bettner and Osborn of Los Angeles, who had agreed to buy the ranch. Details had been arranged, he said, and the sale awaited only the drafting of final legal forms. But the sale fell through. Within the next two months the company borrowed $70,000 from private moneylenders. In March the directors met to authorize their managers Mayo and Walter to sell or lease "any or all of the land belonging to the company." That year another $38,000 was borrowed from banks in San Francisco and Los Angeles.

Under such conditions money was not available for development. Henry had mapped fields for irrigation, but the cost put the plan beyond consideration. Water was a casual item used in a casual way. A little alfalfa grew along the riverbanks where watering could be done by diverting part of a stream. The trees of the carefully laid-out plaza in the town of Newhall had been allowed to die as the water wagon was abandoned.

While the Newhalls had been operating the Rancho San Francisco as a cattle range, the Del Valle family had made the most of the few acres they had retained. Some sixty thousand vines produced grapes which were crushed in Camulos' own small winery on the premises. Ignacio's olive trees were now old

H. G. NEWHALL
President
Los Angeles, Cal.

W. MAYO NEWHALL.
Vice-President
San Francisco, Cal.

GEO. A. NEWHALL
Secretary
San Francisco, Cal.

THE NEWHALL
Land and Farming Co.

OWNERS AND MANAGERS OF

Rancho San Francisco - - **48,611 Acres**
Los Angeles and Ventura Counties

Rancho El Suey - - - **48,834 Acres**
Santa Barbara and San Louis Obispo Counties

Rancho Todos Santos - - **6,987 Acres**
Santa Barbara County

Rancho El Piojo - - - **13,000 Acres**
Monterey County

Rancho San Miguelito - - **22,464 Acres**
Monterey County

Rancho Santa Rita - - - **2,695 Acres**
Monterey County

——AND——

Lands in Santa Clara, San Mateo and Fresno Counties

Offers the selection of Large and Small Tracts on the above
Properties at Moderate Prices and on Liberal Terms

——GENERAL OFFICE——

309 Sansome Street - San Francisco

Los Angeles Office, California Bank Building

enough to produce a good commercial crop; and peach, pear, and apple trees were heavy with fruit. In 1902 Ulpiano del Valle, third son of Ignacio and head of Camulos, decided to extend his orchard to include citrus. The need for more extensive irrigation prompted Don Ulpiano to ask The Newhall Land and Farming Company to formalize an old verbal agreement relative to water use. Delegated to investigate the matter, Mayo found that, since the Del Valles had been using the water for eighteen years, they had acquired a prescriptive right that could not be withdrawn. He also determined there was sufficient water in the Santa Clara River for the existing needs of both interests. An agreement was signed, and Don Ulpiano set out his orange trees adjoining the Newhall grazing lands.

The senior Mrs. Newhall died in 1901, having outlived her husband by nineteen years. Her estate, consisting of various remaining parcels of San Francisco real estate inherited from her husband, and a one-fourth interest in The Newhall Land and Farming Company, was not distributed. Rather than sell the land and distribute the stock, the brothers agreed that it would be better to incorporate their mother's estate and share its income. As a result they formed the White Investment Company and made an equal distribution of the stock. The White Investment Company, which is owned by the heirs of H. M. Newhall, today holds approximately one-third of the stock of The Newhall Land and Farming Company.

XI... *Search for Resources*

I N THE QUARTER-CENTURY that ended in 1904, H. M. Newhall would have noticed little change in the vista of rolling hills and rugged mountains of his ranchos. There had been some expansion in the town of Newhall at the eastern limits of the ranch. The refinery and pipe lines remained as they were in 1879. A branch railroad ran westward through the ranch from Saugus to the coast. The cattle were larger, more uniform, and red instead of black. From the Piojo cattle could reach the train in three days instead of a week; the Suey and Todos Santos ranches lay only a day's trail ride from the cattle cars.

Beginning in late December or January the pale mantle of green, the start of the nourishing grass on which the cattle grazed, appeared suddenly on the hillsides. In good years it would grow lush and remain green until late May; in other years, it would start to turn brown in early April. On a few acres the wild grasses were interspersed with fields of barley. In summer the willows along the streams and the dark oaks and brush on the hillsides supplied the only visible green.

The town of Newhall lay at the southeast corner of a broad valley stretching from the foot of the Tehachapis to San Fernando Pass. A great part of the flatland was covered with oaks, which had led William Manly and other observers to compare the ranch to an English park. Cattle grazed between the oaks and on the barren hills above. From the north the road from San Francisco came down from Fort Tejon on the summit of the Tehachapis, led through San Francisquito Canyon, crossed the valley through Newhall, and continued over San Fernando Pass to Los Angeles. This roadway, deeded to the county, was the origin of today's United States Highway 99 which now crosses the ranch, west of the old road, through Castaic Canyon.

When H. M. Newhall first came to the ranch, the Chinese who had been hired to build the railroad turned their attention to digging gold in Placeritos Canyon and discovered a three-ounce nugget. Twenty-five years later Newhall would have found Placeritos Canyon under lease to a gold-mining company, which failed to produce either a three-ounce nugget or any others.

Mayo had started a cattle-improvement program in the nineties by buying selected bulls from good herds. He gradually accumulated on the Suey Ranch two breeding herds of about fifty head each. One herd was white-faced Herefords; the other, red Durhams. As the black "native cows" passed their prime, they were sold and replaced with larger breeds.

Leases for minerals, oil, and occasional crops were the company's only source of income besides the fluctuating cattle market. This was insufficient to support the growing families of the Newhall sons who had positions of community leadership to maintain.

Aside from his position as major executive of the farming company, Mayo was prominent in San Francisco civic and social affairs. He served for many years as president of the Stanford University board of trustees. His wife, having been educated in Europe, traveled abroad with her son and three daughters to give them the same advantages of a foreign education.

Edwin, who devoted his principal energies to H. M. Newhall & Co., also had four children, two sons and two daughters. His recreation and principal interest was sailing his yacht "Virginia" on the bay, and his massive figure was a familiar sight in bay harbors. At the age of twenty-five he had been elected to fill his father's place on the board of directors of the Bank of California,

72

Henry Mayo Newhall at 50 years (1825-1882).

and he also served as director of several other corporations. As treasurer of the Juvenile Court Committee and president of the California Society for the Prevention of Cruelty to Children, he devoted a considerable amount of time to philanthropic work.

Walter was childless but convivial. He was one of the founders of the California Club in Los Angeles. He delighted in staging elaborate entertainments for his friends' children, hiring clowns from the circus and magicians from the theater to amuse them. One of Walter's friends recalls his presentation of a bear, sculptured in wood, to the California Club, where it stands to this day. The presentation ceremonies followed a gay banquet at which Walter made a speech, as the covering blanket was removed from the bear. A short time later a joker quietly recovered the bear and suggested that it was time for presentation. The forgetful but agreeable Walter made his speech again. After a third delivery of the speech and bear presentation, the guests agreed that the bear should be given honorary membership.

George had not married until two years after his mother's death in 1901, and his two sons were considerably younger than their cousins. His primary interest was H. M. Newhall & Co., which he and his brother Edwin held in partnership. George served as the president of both the San Francisco Fire Commission and the Police Commission, and was suggested for mayor several times. He held office in many clubs, corporations, and charitable organizations.

These civic and social activities called for a comfortable manner of living and uninterrupted contributions of time and money to community and welfare projects. When income was short, the brothers had a source of funds—the inheritance left by their father. From time to time large sums were borrowed from The Newhall Land and Farming Company, which company, in turn, borrowed from banks or other lending agencies. Loans were scrupulously repaid. The funds used to liquidate them usually came from a sale of land or, sometimes, from a timely lease. When land sales fell off, as they usually did in periods of low farm prices, the brothers were worried with debts.

In September 1904 affairs were going badly. The directors, alarmed by continued expenses, instructed the secretary to write to Walter, manager of the Rancho San Francisco, informing him that "it is the sense of this meeting that as the ranch is practically closed up for the season, the payroll is too high and it has got to be run with a smaller crew, the same not to exceed five men, including the superintendent, the cook, the rodeo man, an irrigator, and a helper."

On the Suey Ranch, near Santa Maria, business also shut down after early summer, when the cattle were sold off the dry hills. Therefore, the directors warmly welcomed an offer from the Union Sugar Company, manufacturers of beet sugar, to lease 2,500 acres of the Suey Ranch along the Santa Maria River. By the terms of the lease an annual rent of $5 an acre was provided for land that thirty years before had cost $2 an acre. This meant an annual income of $12,500. In addition the sugar company held an option to buy the land at $52 an acre within four and a half years from the beginning of the lease.

Finances began to improve. A portion of the Santa Rita Ranch, near Salinas, was sold at $50 an acre. The following summer, for the first time in over ten years, a dividend of $4.50 a share, amounting to $40,000, was paid to stockholders. At Christmas each shareholder received a dividend of $2.50 a share.

The earthquake and fire in San Francisco in April 1906 found the family scattered. Mayo Newhall was in San Francisco; his family was traveling in Europe. Mr. and Mrs. George Newhall were also in Europe; their small son George, Jr. was living with a nurse in their Burlingame home. The Edwin Newhall family was home in the Pacific Avenue house. Edwin Newhall was managing the affairs of H. M. Newhall & Co., which had recently moved into its new building on Battery Street.

The day before the earthquake Edwin Newhall, Jr. had taken his two sisters to Carmel to visit friends and then proceeded to the Suey Ranch. He had recently been graduated from Massachusetts Agricultural College and was learning the ranch business from the ground up. Delegated to herd a dozen or more horses from the Suey to the Rancho San Francisco the next day, he arrived in Santa Maria at noon and learned about the earthquake. He turned the horses over to another hand and immediately started for Guadalupe to catch the northbound coast train. The train carried him as far as Salinas where a railroad bridge had been shifted by the earthquake and had blocked passage of the train. He was forced to board a southbound train to Los Angeles where he found that his uncle Walter had a reservation for that night on the valley train to San Francisco. Walter, who was ailing, gave Edwin his place.

San Francisco was ablaze when the train pulled in the next morning. Blackened ruins lay between flames from the waterfront back through the hills. Young Edwin made his way home to find only a man who was cleaning up plaster and broken bric-a-brac tossed down by the earthquake. His parents and brother Almer had gone to the Presidio to camp out when the flames had advanced to within a few blocks of their Pacific Avenue house. During the day the wind changed and the Edwin Newhall family, augmented by some of the staff of H. M. Newhall & Co. who had lost their homes, moved back to Pacific Avenue.

The following day Edwin Newhall put up a sign on his residence: "H. M. Newhall & Co." For the next two months the Edwin Newhall home doubled as offices for H. M. Newhall & Co. and The Newhall Land and Farming Company. By midsummer the downtown building was replaced with a temporary structure and both companies' permanent records, which had been recovered intact, were moved there.

Walter Newhall's health did not improve. In the fall of 1906 he closed his Los Angeles house and went to Europe with his wife to try to recuperate. He was in England only a week or two before doctors advised him to return home. On Christmas Day, at the age of forty-six, he died in San Francisco. His estate, consisting of his shares in The Newhall Land and Farming Company and White Investment Company, and a small orange grove at Duarte, was left in trust to provide an income for his wife and, on her death, an inheritance for his thirteen nieces and nephews. His wife died thirty-six years later.

Surviving Walter were only three of the five Newhall brothers. Meanwhile some of the third generation had grown up. To the board of directors, consisting of George, president, Mayo, vice-president and general manager, and Edwin, secretary, were added Edwin's two sons. Almer, the elder, was a Yale graduate who had joined the firm of H. M. Newhall & Co. Edwin, Jr., after his college training for ranch work, spent a year as cow hand on the Suey. He later worked on the Rancho San Francisco, was Mayo's assistant in the general administrative office, and for two years was superintendent of the Suey. Of the third generation, only Edwin, Jr. was primarily interested in and trained for the ranch business. At this writing he has been associated with the company as employee, officer, and director for fifty-three years.

Unlike some of the other large California landholders who were involved in running feuds with railroads and utility companies, the Newhalls always welcomed transit over their land by public utilities. Easements and rights of way for railroads, county roads, electric power and telephone lines were granted for nominal sums. In June 1875, a few months after the purchase of the Rancho San Francisco, H. M. Newhall deeded a right of way, eight miles long and totaling one hundred acres, to the Southern Pacific Company for the consideration of one dollar. For the same price Newhall deeded 426 acres to the railroad subsidiary for the town of Newhall, and for later spurs and extensions. This policy of accessibility was continued by his sons, who realized that communication, transport, and power increased ease of operations as well as land values.

In 1908, when the city of Los Angeles stretched its arm 250 miles north to get Owens Valley water for the parched city dwellers, the planned route for the giant aqueduct lay across the Rancho San Francisco. The aqueduct was to come in from the Mojave Desert and down San Francisquito Canyon, where a small creek, flowing from the northeast, fed the Santa Clara River. One of the city's reservoirs was to be constructed behind the St. Francis Dam in San Francisquito Canyon to store water and generate power. From there the great aqueduct was to cross the eastern end of the ranch and extend over San Fernando Pass to the spillway above San Fernando Reservoir.

The directors readily agreed to an easement for the passage of Owens Valley water through the ranch and also gave permission, during periods of excess water, for reservoir spillage into the Santa Clara River for ranch use. Construction of the St. Francis Dam was to beget a disaster which later proved to be a milestone in the history of the Rancho San Francisco and The Newhall Land and Farming Company.

During this period various oil leases were executed on the San Francisco Ranch; they all had one thing in common—no oil. As leases expired on the rolling land east and south of the town of Newhall, the land was sold and the money paid out in dividends. One of the oil companies negotiated a lease at $4,000 a year for an area on the Todos Santos Ranch. After exploration proved unsuccessful, the oil company forgot about the lease, but once a year a check for $4,000 was received at the Newhall office. This continued for many years until a sharp-eyed accountant discovered the annual payment on the oil company's books and the lease was canceled.

Though the oil companies were disappointed in the outcome of their leases on Newhall land, there was one happy lessee. The Union Sugar Company found that beets grew magnificently on the valley land at the Suey Ranch, and decided to exercise their option to buy the 2,560 acres they had under lease. Early in 1909 the sugar company made a down payment of $30,000 and just before Christmas paid the balance of $105,000. These capital funds were paid out to the stockholders, and dividends were raised to the rate of $1 a share per month.

It was the dividend policy of The Newhall Land and Farming Company that disqualified the company as a successful business enterprise. Regardless of the source from which money was received, the balance, after payment of bills, was distributed in dividends. It made no difference whether it was received from cattle operations or from sale of land. There were no income tax complications to make necessary the separation of capital sales from operations. The continuation of such a policy would have meant the liquidation of the company.

Mayo Newhall raised the first objection to this policy when the land on the Suey Ranch was sold to Union Sugar. He had watched the progress of the sugar company's irrigation project and opposed the sale. He insisted that some of the money be used to buy additional land and that the policy of liquidation be reversed. About this time the Fryer and McGuire tracts, both part of the old Rancho Simi which adjoined the Rancho San

Francisco at the top of the mountains to the south, were put on the market by the Union Oil Company. The oil company retained the mineral rights, and for $31,500 The Newhall Land and Farming Company bought the surface rights to ten thousand acres of steep, hilly grazing land.

To meet a distribution of $10,000 a month in dividends, the company had to look for other sources of money. The Giambastiani Fuel and Feed Company of Los Angeles called attention to an asset that had been overlooked: the magnificent stand of several thousand oak trees in the parklike upper valley. From October 1910 through 1912 the woodsmen spared no trees, which were bought at $1 a cord and reduced to charcoal for the bakeries of Los Angeles. Income continued to be forthcoming from the sale of small parcels of land. The remaining 550 acres of Soto's Santa Rita Ranch, which had produced nothing but light grain crops, were sold for $100 an acre to a Salinas buyer; and a sale of thirty-six acres in Menlo Park brought $5,000. The Rancho San Francisco was again offered for sale in small parcels.

In the spring of 1912 Mayo Newhall called the attention of the directors to the Del Valle property. A few years earlier the first citrus trees in the Santa Clara Valley had been set out on the Rancho Camulos. This grove of oranges and lemons had thrived and proved profitable. The directors agreed that Mayo could buy tools and trees to start an orchard, and in May 1912 he signed a contract for five thousand orange and lemon trees to be delivered in May or June of the following year. An orchard camp was established adjoining Camulos at the extreme west end of the San Francisco Ranch some nine miles down-river from the ranch headquarters. About 115 acres were planted with oranges and 35 acres with lemons. The citrus orchards opened up a new way of life to The Newhall Land and Farming Company. Cattle and rentals were no longer the company's only source of income. They had cultivated the land and made it productive.

Farming in California was entering a new era, an era that prescribed the importation of water to irrigate the arid lands. The Newhall ranches had been run in about the same way as the Mexican rancheros had operated, with little change in more than sixty years. The large-scale irrigation of a commercial crop meant the end of the rancho and the beginning of modern farming.

A result of this new way of thinking was the purchase of the Markley Ranch. The estate of John Markley of Marysville was selling two thousand acres of flatland in the center of the Sacramento Valley, west of Marysville. No purchase could have been in greater contrast with the traditional Newhall holdings, which uniformly consisted of Spanish land grants in the southern part of the Coast Range. Every winter the waters of the Sacramento River flooded the Markley Ranch, and most of the land was covered with tules and other marshy growth. By clearing and draining 160 acres, Markley was able to produce a fine crop of beans on land that had been made extremely rich by the annual flooding. The Newhalls and another prospective buyer bid $40 an acre and bought the property jointly. A short time later the Newhall company came into possession of the entire two thousand acres. The land was cleared of tules, leveled, and rented to local farmers on a share-crop basis, and the production of highly profitable bean crops began.

In 1913 the company made what its directors for many years declared to be a "remarkable sale." The inactive Newhall Oil & Development Company, launched thirteen years earlier by Gilbert Palache, continued to hold title to a tract of about fifteen hundred acres adjoining Camulos at the west end of the San Francisco Ranch. The land had been leased at various times to different oil companies including the Eureka Oil Company and Standard Oil Company. No oil had been discovered. A group of Swiss oil men appeared on the scene and asked for an option on the fifteen hundred acres at the staggering price of $100,000. The Newhall Land and Farming Company hastily arranged cancellation of existing leases, dissolved The Newhall Oil & Development Company, "bought" back the land, and sold it to the Swiss group. From today's vantage point it was a "remarkable *buy*," for now the tract is a forest of oil derricks.

Edwin W. Newhall, third son of Henry M. Newhall, died in October 1915. His two sons Almer and Edwin, Jr. remained on the board of directors of The Newhall Land and Farming Company with their uncles Mayo and George. Mayo's son

79

William Mayo, Jr. was elected a fifth member of the board. The third generation was now in a majority.

World War I had started, and the demand for food meant a need for the products of The Newhall Land and Farming Company. However, the surplus in the treasury was soon taken up with taxes and increased labor expenses, and wartime profits barely maintained the flow of funds to which the growing Newhall family had become accustomed. In 1922, just before the postwar recession set in, the company made its first major sale. The land sold was the Piojo (the combined Piojo and San Miguelito), the first ranch bought by Henry Mayo Newhall.

The Piojo had been satisfactorily operated as a breeding ranch, supporting more than fifteen hundred cows, but roads and railroads had passed it by. At this time a long three days on the trail were required to drive the weanlings to King City for shipment, as trucking of cattle had not yet been developed. Communications had simplified life on the other ranches, but the Piojo was still in the wilderness.

Wilderness land was the requirement of the Piedmont Land & Cattle Company, owned by William Randolph Hearst. Hearst wanted to add the Piojo to his vast San Simeon estates and offered $30 an acre, or $1,150,000, for the land, improvements, and livestock. The offer was accepted. Twenty years later the Hearst interests also lost the Piojo. It was bought by the United States Army to serve as part of Camp Hunter Liggett. Its hills and grazing lands became infantry training grounds, and the ranch houses were converted into officers' quarters.

The company also tried to sell the Markley Ranch. The postwar recession had arrived, and armies were no longer demanding beans. The directors voted to sell the Markley "as soon as possible, in one or two tracts, at not less than $100 an acre." But money was scarce in 1924, and the Newhall company found no buyers.

The desire to sell land was becoming a motivating influence. In good farming years the directors had distributed all available cash in dividends; when bad years came along, they had no reserve. In 1918 and 1919 they had constantly refused offers for their land. The American Beet Sugar Company had leased and offered to buy all the flatland on the Rancho San Francisco, and had spent $85,000 on an irrigation system. In the third year of tenancy an influx of the beet leaf hopper ruined the crop, and the sugar company surrendered its lease. The Newhalls felt obliged to refund the money spent on the irrigation system. Thus the company confronted the postwar years with no money and with their potential buyers lost.

In 1924 Mayo's son-in-law Arthur Chesebrough joined the five-man board of directors, taking the seat vacated by William Mayo Newhall, Jr. who had resigned to enter the diplomatic service. Chesebrough had started working as a young man in his family's shipping business. During World War I he had visited the Rancho San Francisco with his wife Elizabeth and two small sons and decided he would stay. From orchard assistant he had risen to the position of superintendent of the ranch when he joined the Newhall board of directors. He immediately urged an increase of production by adding to irrigated lands. Wells were being drilled and in several instances tenants had installed irrigation systems in lieu of payment of rentals.

As a flood control measure, the state bought about two hundred acres of the Markley Ranch to install a by-pass. For a period of two years after the completion of the mile-wide by-pass, the land dried up and only barley could be raised. Then the company made an agreement with the state to allow pumping of water over the levees that bordered the by-pass, and beans were grown again.

With the late twenties came a period of "lasting prosperity," and it was generally conceded that good times had come to stay. The ranches were in good shape. New irrigation works were progressing; cattle prices were high; new oil leases, at excellent rates, had been signed for lands along the Santa Clara River. Land values soared. The annual payments received from the Hearst company for the Piojo Ranch were distributed as dividends. It was expected that future sales would be even better. Although salaries and bonuses were liberal, the directors voted to pay themselves ten per cent of the net profits each year. The family custom of borrowing from the company, a practice followed for nearly forty years, had become a habit.

When The Newhall Land and Farming Company was organized in 1883, it was incorporated for fifty years. Various acts of the directors over the years indicated that they thought it would be dissolved upon the death of the last of Henry Mayo Newhall's sons. When funds received from the sale of the Piojo had been exhausted, other land could be sold. But disaster is part of the story of any long-range human endeavor, and disaster lay ahead.

XII... *Disaster and Depression*

T MIDNIGHT, March 12, 1928, the lights went out on the Rancho San Francisco. No one was aware of the failure, as everyone was asleep. Farther down the valley in Fillmore and Santa Paula people still on the streets saw the street lights black out, and late lunch stands and gas stations plunged into darkness. Calls were put in to the Southern California Edison Company. An hour and a quarter later, after having tried vainly to rouse their men at the power station at St. Francis Dam, investigators sent out by the company relayed the awful news: the dam had burst.

Some people in the area had been nervous about recurrent seepages of muddy water from the dam, but only the day before William Mulholland, the engineer who had built the whole Owens Valley water system, had inspected the leaks and decided that they were harmless. The dam had been built, unknowingly, against hillsides whose composition was not suitable to support such a concrete structure. The pressure of thirty-four thousand acre-feet of water was too much, and the dam gave way all at once. A sixty-foot wall of water came crashing through the canyon and thundered down the valley of the Santa Clara at a speed of eighteen miles an hour, sweeping everything before it.

There was no warning for the people on the ranch. Houses, trees, power lines, automobiles—everything in the path of the flood—were swept away. Castaic Junction was inundated. Four ranch families were drowned; others were saved when they were borne to safety on floating objects. Near the lower end of the ranch the Southern California Edison Company had a work camp of 140 men, sleeping in tents near the river bed. Eighty-four of these men were lost. Farther down the valley, at Fillmore, Santa Paula, and Oxnard, state troopers, police, and telephone operators labored heroically to save the inhabitants, and most were able to escape to higher ground.

The flood was quickly over, but a count revealed that 385 people had been lost. Over 1,200 houses were destroyed, and vast acres of farmland damaged. On the Rancho San Francisco irrigation pipes and pumps were demolished. Most of the irrigable land was covered with sand to depths varying from a few inches to many feet. Bridges, buildings, and orchards were a tangled litter.

The city of Los Angeles, assuming full responsibility for the disaster, appointed a commission to negotiate all damage claims. The commission paid out a total of $15,000,000, and no case was ever taken to court. The Newhall Land and Farming Company, owners of the largest single area in the path of the flood, filed the largest property damage claim. A little over two years later, in June 1930, the company was awarded $737,039.59. The money was to be paid at a later date.

The damage to fields, grazing lands, buildings, and crops had come at the peak of the period of prosperity. Before the company could start rehabilitation, the Great Depression arrived. It began with the stock market crash of October 29, 1929, and from the financial centers it spread outward, effecting a creeping paralysis through the entire economy. The Newhall family companies did not at first realize the full impact of the depression.

On December 22, 1929, seven weeks after the stock market collapse, George Newhall, youngest of the five sons of H. M. Newhall, died at sixty-seven. He had been president of The Newhall Land and Farming Company and White Investment Company. He had also been a partner, with his nephew Almer, in the firm of H. M. Newhall & Co., which, as treasurer, handled all of the financial affairs of the family businesses.

The only surviving son of H. M. Newhall was Mayo. Now in his late seventies, Mayo had long been the operating head of the farming company. A few years earlier he had lost his eyesight while undergoing surgery but, despite his affliction and age, he remained cheerful and clear-headed in keeping watch over the details of ranch operations. Suddenly he felt old and helpless when he learned, after the death of his youngest brother George, that H. M. Newhall & Co. was in a near-bankrupt condition. Suspecting that The Newhall Land and Farming Company to which he had devoted his life was in jeopardy, Mayo sought the counsel of Atholl McBean, the husband of his eldest daughter Margaret.

McBean was an experienced executive. After two years at Hotchkiss School in Lakeville, Connecticut, he had gone to work in the clay products business that his father had founded as a copartnership in 1875. Starting as a day laborer at a wage of $32 a month, McBean had intensive training in all operations of the business. In 1923 he became president and supervised the company's development into a publicly owned stock corporation. At forty McBean was president of the San Francisco Chamber of Commerce and a director of a dozen major corporations. The force of his personality was enhanced by his impressive stature. He was fifty-one when he was asked by his father-in-law at a meeting in San Francisco on August 27, 1930, to look into the muddled affairs of The Newhall Land and Farming Company. What he discovered was disheartening.

When George Newhall died, he and his nephew and surviving partner Almer were heavily in debt, principally to the Bank of California. Their assets comprised a portfolio of nearly worthless stock and the funds that the partnership held as treasurer of The Newhall Land and Farming Company and White Investment Company. Almer forfeited all of his possessions, and H. M. Newhall & Co. declared bankruptcy. H. M. Newhall & Co., acting as bankers for The Newhall Land and Farming Company and White Investment Company, had on deposit about $280,000, which was immediately seized by the Bank of California, thus depriving the companies of all free cash. Had each company deposited its money in banks, the funds could not have been appropriated. According to a statement on file, dated October 17, 1930, the total indebtedness of H. M. Newhall & Co., its partners, and the companies owned by them, exclusive of commercial accounts, was $3,091,686.40. Of this sum $494,220.24

was owed to The Newhall Land and Farming Company. The stated net worth of H. M. Newhall & Co. was $426,598.17.

Aside from wishing to be of personal help to its members, McBean was interested in the affairs of H. M. Newhall & Co. and its affiliates because he hoped ultimately to collect from the firm the amount owed to The Newhall Land and Farming Company. As time passed and the depression intensified, it became increasingly evident that there was no hope of collecting the notes due.

McBean's ardor for facts was thwarted when he found that the books of account had always been kept on a cash receipt and disbursement basis and that it was impossible to obtain financial statements of any value. Although his recommendation to appoint a comptroller was at first vigorously opposed, authorization was finally given for the employment on November 1, 1930, of an accountant to install a new accounting system.

While no investigation of the records prior to 1905 was made, it was revealed that there had been intercompany borrowings as early as that time and that it had been a continuing practice. It was apparent that for many years the members of the family had not only been living beyond their regular income but beyond that received from the distribution of capital assets.

In 1931 a combined statement was compiled from the financial accounts of The Newhall Land and Farming Company and its affiliates and the White Investment Company and its affiliates for the ten-year period ending December 31, 1931. The statement showed the following:

Profits from sale of real estate	$1,179,594.53
Other income, before deducting executive salaries and bonuses (intercompany income eliminated)	1,305,506.42
Total	$2,485,100.95
Executive salaries and bonuses	$ 810,200.00
Dividends (intercompany dividends eliminated)	1,718,828.56
Total	$2,529,028.56
Excess of expenditures, including dividends	$ 43,927.61

In addition to this, during the same period a total of $603,240 received from sales of various ranches was paid as liquidating dividends. A sum of $1,125,000 from the sale of the Piojo Ranch in 1922, plus interest at six per cent amounting to $269,720.22, had been received by The Newhall Land and Farming Company in annual sums during the years 1922 and 1923 and from 1926 to 1931. The receipt of these payments in such substantial amounts over a period of years undoubtedly had a great deal to do with the overexpansion of the personal activities of the family.

The two final payments of $100,000 each for the Piojo Ranch were received in 1930 and 1931. On November 7, 1930, The Newhall Land and Farming Company received a check for $737,039.59 from the city of Los Angeles for damages caused by the bursting of the St. Francis Dam. These receipts enabled the farming company to pay all of its debts, including interest, during the month of November 1930. Thus fate was to mollify the disaster of March 1928 by providing the funds urgently needed to save the company.

The new accounting system had been designed and made effective as of January 1, 1932, and the company's first financial statement, received in the spring of 1933, revealed a loss of $126,000. The statement for the year 1933, completed in the spring of 1934, revealed a further loss of $71,300. These discouraging results indicated the necessity for immediate action to re-establish the properties on an earning basis.

McBean, new to the ranch business, asked for the help and co-operation of directors, officers, and employees. He obtained the board of directors' consent to employ an expert to give advice on how best to develop the land. In that capacity he engaged Joseph McGrath, a rancher from Oxnard.

A more knowledgeable person than McGrath could hardly have been found to advise the company. He was the son of an Irish immigrant, Dominic McGrath, who during the drought of the 1860's had abandoned his sheep ranch, comprising the present sites of Berkeley and the University of California. He drove south in a buckboard and bought land at Oxnard near the mouth of the Santa Clara River. Joseph McGrath was born there in 1878 —the year that H. M. Newhall planted his first wheat crop forty miles up the river. When his father died in 1908 Joseph McGrath became president of the Dominic McGrath Estate Company and held the position until the company was dissolved in 1950. He acquired properties so wisely and farmed so well that the company, at the time of its dissolution, was worth $4,000,000. McGrath looked over the Newhall properties and early in 1935 submitted his opinion: with proper investment of $500,000 in development over a two-year period, the ranches could be made profitable.

Some of the members of the board of directors took the view that the land should be sold and the company liquidated. McBean reviewed the matter with a member of a San Francisco accounting firm, John Forbes, who expressed the thought that they would not realize more than three million dollars from a sale. Through J. J. Hunter of the Bank of California, the management requested Fickett and Houchin, who had liquidated vast properties for Miller & Lux, to submit an estimate of the liquidating value. Their appraisal agreed exactly with Forbes's evaluation.

McBean was so confident that the properties could be managed profitably that he was successful in persuading the board of directors to pursue this course rather than to countenance liquidation. He had endeavored to borrow money from the Bank of California and had been refused credit. The Crocker First National Bank was the only avenue open, but his request there met with great resistance from the committee on loans. The committee took the position that, because McBean had been instrumental in effecting the consolidation of the Crocker Bank and the First National Bank, he was trading on his friendship with the Crocker family in trying to influence an agricultural loan that the bank did not approve. Nevertheless, he was successful in securing a commitment for $250,000, which he decided to accept, knowing that if the company could make a satisfactory start it would not be difficult to secure an additional sum of $250,000 later.

The low point reached by the company in 1933 coincided with the fiftieth anniversary of the company's founding. But in foreseeing the dissolution of their company in fifty years, the Newhall sons had not taken into account the foresight and shrewdness of a new generation. The recovery and restoration of the Newhall fortune was to be spectacular.

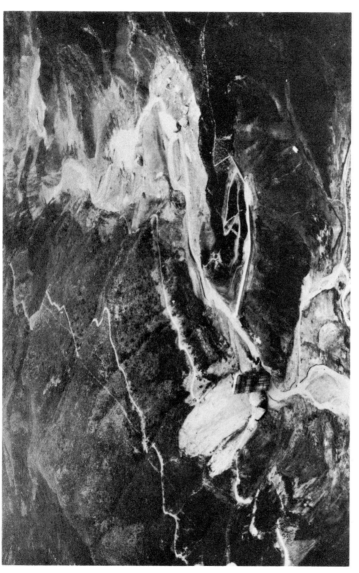

Air view of St. Francis Dam after 1928 disaster, looking southeast. Fault shown on bank to west of central section or "Tombstone" left standing. From copy of Report of Committee . . . of Los Angeles to Investigate . . . Failure of the St. Francis Dam. Huntington Library Collections.

XIII...*Oil*

HE STORY of a family company falls naturally into the framework of generations. In the Newhall family Henry Mayo Newhall was the builder. He had assembled both a fortune and a stake in the future. The second generation regarded the company as their father's estate, to be liquidated and distributed when possible or necessary. At the time of Henry Newhall's death his assets were valued at between $2,500,000 and $3,000,000. The twenty-three separate parcels of San Francisco real estate and improvements, the Piojo and San Miguelito ranches, the Santa Rita or "Los Gatos" Ranch and the sixty lots in the town of Santa Rita, and all the remaining assets passing under Henry Newhall's will were sold and the proceeds disbursed. Fifty years after his death the remaining ranch properties were appraised at $3,000,000. During their tenure the second generation had developed farming, improved the cattle, and maintained company unity.

The third generation is the period in which many family companies draw their final breath. Different family groups go their different ways; accidents, inheritance, or personal considerations often throw the power of decision into hands that are unqualified or untrained. Twelve of Henry Mayo Newhall's grandchildren lived to adulthood; six were grandsons. Henry's son Donald was a portrait painter who divided his time between New York and Europe. Mayo's son William Mayo, Jr. was in the diplomatic service in Peking. George's sons George, Jr. and Walter were still in their twenties at the time disaster struck. Edwin's two sons Edwin, Jr. and Almer had long served on the board of directors of the family companies. Almer, broken by the collapse of H. M. Newhall & Co., died in 1933 at fifty-one. Mayo Newhall, long the head of the company and the last surviving son of its founder, died in December 1934 at the age of eighty. The third generation was in charge.

Edwin W. Newhall, Jr. found himself the only Newhall on the board of directors. Atholl McBean, vigorously working to salvage the company, took his father-in-law's place as president. Arthur Chesebrough, a widower in failing health, had resigned. Other directors were Fentress Hill, who had married Mayo's second daughter Marion; J. J. Hunter, president of the Bank of California; John Forbes, accountant and economist; and lawyers Edgar Zook and O. C. Cushing. The company was no longer one man's family.

When Joseph McGrath was appointed to succeed Arthur Chesebrough as assistant to the president, he brought in as his own assistant George E. Bushell, who had been superintendent on the McGrath properties. Bushell, a sixteen-year-old Irish immigrant, had arrived in Los Angeles in 1909 with only five cents and a letter of introduction. The letter had paved his way to a job as a hand on the McGrath ranches, where he had remained, with the exception of two years of World War I army service, learning the business from bottom to top.

Under direction of these two experienced men, The Newhall Land and Farming Company began its long uphill climb. The Crocker quarter-million-dollar loan was invested in wells, pumps, tractors, and other equipment to put the land under intense cultivation. The lemon orchard, which had not prospered on the dry west end of the ranch, was replanted with oranges.

During these busy months McBean was in occasional conversation with Patrick Calhoun. Calhoun, a former corporation lawyer and founder of the street railway system in San Francisco, had been a highly controversial figure during the municipal graft investigations in San Francisco twenty-eight years earlier. He was a giant of a man, spectacular in appearance, and possessed the courtly manner of his native South. At eighty, dignified and personable, he complained that, although he had made several fortunes in his life, he had lost each one and had nothing to leave to his seven children. The Barnsdall Oil Company of Los Angeles gave him another chance. His assignment was to call on Atholl McBean in San Francisco to negotiate a lease on what was known as the Potrero section of the Rancho San Francisco.

The Potrero comprises a succession of rolling hills, bisected by a deep canyon, on the southern border of the Rancho San Francisco. On the south side of the hills, off the ranch, is Pico Canyon, where the first producing oil well in California was drilled. Since 1864 oil leases had been a dominant activity on the Rancho San Francisco. The valley of the Santa Clara, where seepages of tar had been noted by the earliest explorers and had been gathered for fuel by mission friars, was considered by every oil company to have geological possibility. Over the years some fifty different companies had leased portions of the ranch, but many of these leases expired before the land had been drilled. Both Union Oil and Associated Oil had drilled to a depth of over five thousand feet without success. Before 1934 Mayo Newhall wrote: "There is no indication that this ranch is an oil property."

McBean was reluctant, in view of this unproductive history, to tie up ranch lands in a fruitless search. But a lease, even without oil, was a source of income, and the Potrero was range land, distant from planned irrigation and development projects. Calhoun was successful in negotiating the lease.

Affairs on the ranches looked more promising. Every cent of income was plowed back into debt retirement or into land development. Tenants, who for years had done most of the actual farming on a share-crop basis, were informed that after 1935 The Newhall Land and Farming Company would work its own land.

The breeding of calves, long the company's major business, had not gone well since the sale of the Piojo Ranch. Cattle prices had dropped to an unexpected low of three to four cents a pound, and it was cheaper to buy calves than to breed them. The amount of land needed to support two cows for a year could fatten five calves through the eight-month grass season. The answer was to discontinue breeding, buy yearlings on the market, pasture them when grass was available, and build feed pens to fatten them for the higher-priced market. Construction of a $5,000 feed mill got under way.

After losses of $126,000 in 1932 and $71,000 in 1933, the company finally moved into the black in 1934. For that year the statement showed an operating profit of $24,303. This income was derived entirely from farming and cattle operations and, in that depression year, gave indication that the new operating policy was beginning to bear fruit. Each of the following two years brought profits from ranch operations in excess of $100,000. In February 1936 the company resumed the payment of dividends, which had been discontinued in 1932. The investment in the land was proving sound.

On August 10, 1936, a drill started boring into the sage-covered ground in Potrero Canyon. The hole under the drill shaft was christened "Rancho San Francisco No. 1." The Barnsdall Oil Company had not made an important discovery in eight years, but hope springs eternal among wildcatters.

On December 23, 1936, a present arrived in the form of an announcement from the Barnsdall Oil Company that the drill bit had struck rich oil sands at 6,100 feet. The Newhall Land and Farming Company declared a Christmas dividend. Work, planning, and diligence had saved the company. The oil was an unexpected bonus.

The drilling of RSF No. 1 continued beyond the oil sands that were hit in December, and soon the well was flowing 118 barrels a day, which was considered to be a good average yield. No. 1 was later deepened twice and each time production was increased. Less than a year later the second well, completed at 6,713 feet, produced 631 barrels a day. The oil field was a major discovery. Petroleum engineers and consulting geologists joined the staff of The Newhall Land and Farming Company to advise the landowners on how to protect their interests and their oil reserves.

As the Barnsdall Company continued drilling, the field grew, and by 1944 the company was drilling its forty-fourth well. Until then the wells had touched what are known now as the "upper zones," striking oil at an average depth of a mile and a quarter underground. However, new drilling techniques were making deep drilling feasible. RSF No. 44 hit a new oil pool more than two miles underground. Well No. 66, drilled a couple of years later, became one of the deepest producing wells in the world and opened up still another pool.

After the Barnsdall discovery there was a rush for oil leases on the Rancho San Francisco. One of the new lessees, the Humble Oil Company, looking westward from Texas in 1948 for new oil sites, had drilled thirteen dry holes in various southern California locations and had made only one strike, so minor as to be without commercial value. Humble took a lease near Castaic Junction in the dry bed of the Santa Clara River and adjoining hill slopes to the south. In January 1950 the oil company brought in its first well on the Rancho San Francisco. More wells were drilled in strategic locations to feel out the limits of the field. The seventh well came in on December 18, 1951, at the excellent rate of 704 barrels a day. It was the major strike of the year in the state of California.

Each year oil production on the Newhall Ranch (as the Rancho San Francisco is now known) has increased. The Newhall-Potrero field, which became the leasehold of the Sunray Mid-Continent Oil Company when that company acquired the Barnsdall Oil Company, apparently reached its peak in March 1955, three years later than geologists had estimated. Drilling, however, continued into the deeper zones and early in 1957, twenty years and one month after the first discovery, RSF No. 143 was brought in, with a flow of about 600 barrels a day.

In 1955 a major new oil pool was discovered on the Los Angeles County Honor Farm on land adjoining United States Highway 99, north of Castaic Junction. The Honor Farm occupied land which had been sold in the twenties by The Newhall Land and Farming Company and was later bought by the county for a minimum-security prison. The county's new bonanza adjoined the boundaries of the Newhall Ranch and enabled the

Newhall company to lease some of its land along that boundary in 1956 to the Texas and Superior oil companies. Production from the first two wells exceeded expectations. Drilling continues to this day.

In the barren Potrero Canyon, where Newhall cattle graze between oil rigs, is a large silver-painted plant filled with humming motors and surrounded by a forest of pipes and tanks. It is a repressuring plant that forces the natural gas from the oil wells back into the pool, thereby causing the oil to flow to the surface under pressure, a more efficient method of recovery than pumping.

Every barrel of oil meant money in the treasury of The Newhall Land and Farming Company and provided the means with which to implement and accelerate the company's new philosophy of operation. Ranch development was well under way before oil was discovered. Recovery, even in the years of low farm income, had been gratifying. As early as 1935 McBean was looking over ranch properties offered for sale. He pointed to the fact that in the thirty years from 1908 to 1939 some $3,000,000 had been realized from sale of company lands and that practically the entire proceeds had been disbursed in salaries and dividends. Henry Mayo Newhall's estate had been undergoing slow liquidation.

Land was no longer something to be sold. The directors voted approval of a policy of land replacement. The family company was no longer an estate to be distributed; it was a corporation organized to produce, develop, and grow. Funds to support this decision were supplied when the company was forced to sell the Todos Santos Ranch. In 1942 the United States government was looking for training camp sites for a wartime army. Government attorneys told The Newhall Land and Farming Company that the Todos Santos would fit the army's needs, and gave the company a choice of negotiating a sale or having the property taken over by the exercise of eminent domain. The Todos Santos was renamed Camp Cooke. The money received from the sale was set aside for "land replacement." The Newhall company retained mineral rights, and occasional oil leases were executed, but at this writing there has been no discovery.

From 1939 to 1952 the American farmer caught up with, and in many cases surpassed, the income level of the American public. Crop and cattle prices were at all-time highs. The Newhall company, over a twenty-year period, reinvested a major portion of its oil profits in land and improvements. The result has been the development of the company into one of the leading western land operations. As the *californios*, the gold seekers, and the merchant-railroad men were typical of their day, so is the present operation of The Newhall Land and Farming Company representative of the revolution in twentieth-century western agriculture. Expansion, mechanization, and a different social outlook are all part of the new picture. Without oil, the program would have been carried forward, but more slowly and on a smaller scale. The revenue from oil not only gave free rein to creative experiments but new outlets for productive energy.

XIV... *Cattle and Oranges*

OSEPH MCGRATH resigned from the Newhall company in 1939. His own large-scale ranch operations had grown too demanding. He left behind his long-time assistant George Bushell. Bushell, first as general manager and then as president of The Newhall Land and Farming Company, never relaxed his constant drive for development.

Cattle raising had been the traditional activity of The Newhall Land and Farming Company, and cattle, also, were an important part of the new era. The rebuilding program launched in the early thirties gave priority to the construction of feed pens and a feed mill. In 1940 the company decided that it could feed not only its own cattle, but that it should go into the business of fattening cattle for others.

Today as many as twenty thousand head of cattle each year are fattened in the feed pens on the sloping hillside adjoining Henry Mayo Newhall's original house. There the cattle, mostly white-faced Herefords, are fed on a carefully balanced ration mixed in the adjoining mill operated by electronic controls. An ingredient of the ration typifies the profitable use of waste products. The peel of juice oranges from the company's groves is ground up and helps supply vitamins to the cattle. In return manure from the feed pens is used to fertilize the orange trees.

A total of 2,375 head of sheep were among the assets transferred under the will of Henry Mayo Newhall, and originally the Rancho San Francisco had been used for sheep grazing. In the interest of diversification the decade from 1935 to 1945 again found sheep on Newhall land. After 1945, as the pasture land gradually was put under irrigation and used for crops, the sheep operation was discontinued.

A brief experiment in hog raising on the Newhall Ranch was more unfortunate. In 1939 Bushell took advantage of the sale of a purebred herd of Poland Chinas by the McGrath Estate Company. A little mathematics indicated that a herd of four hundred gilts, averaging two litters per year and six pigs per litter, could produce forty-eight hundred butchering hogs a year.

The pig pens were not far from the original Newhall house, in which lived Henry Poole, the feed yard superintendent, and his wife. While management was figuring its future profits, Mrs. Poole turned her hand to verse and sent her composition to George Bushell:

> I'm haunted and helpless and under the spell
> Of that strangely elusive, exotic smell.
> At night when the moon and the stars brightly shine
> Its fragrance permeates me like heady old wine.
> No door or window or wall of tin
> Can keep that odor from seeping in.
> Though my life has become a living nightmare,
> Though I rant and rave and tear my hair,
> The price of pork still continues to rise
> And the cute little piggy just multiplies.
> Someone gets rich and it isn't me—
> I only get rich in profanity.
> But the one who is guilty of causing this grief
> Is the smiling George Bushell, Commander-in-Chief.

Fortune, in the shape of management's misfortune, soon smiled on the long-suffering Mrs. Poole. In the spring of 1940, when the herd had been built to breeding proportions, a form of hoof-and-mouth disease killed three hundred pigs, set breeding time back for the remainder, and left the herd emaciated. By fall another three hundred head from the first crop of small pigs died of cholera, despite a careful vaccination program. Having started under a cloud, the operation was made even more unprofitable when toward the end of the year the price of pork fell and the price of barley, on which the hogs fed, began to rise. The company went out of the hog business.

After 1935 the policy of discontinuing the breeding of calves was actively carried out. When World War II ended and a drop in the cattle market was foreseen, the purchase of high-priced calves to sell on a falling market became an increasing risk. A breeding operation appeared to be the only way to avert a possible loss, and a search was made for a suitable ranch.

In 1947 management inspected the New Columbia Ranch, comprising 6,150 acres on the west side of the San Joaquin Valley near Firebaugh. The ranch had water rights and irrigated pasture, but the land appeared to be too alkaline for anything but cattle. In November 1947 the New Columbia, stocked with nearly two thousand head of black Aberdeen Angus cattle, became the property of The Newhall Land and Farming Company. On closer observation the appearance of the land was strongly suggestive of the Markley Ranch.

The Markley, totaling two thousand acres when it was bought in 1912, had been reduced by sales in the twenties to about twelve hundred acres. When the by-pass built by the state had stopped the annual flooding, the Newhall company and some of the neighboring farms joined to form an irrigation district. Production of rice, beets, and lima beans under controlled irrigation was successful enough to dictate a policy of expansion when adjacent land came on the market. The Markley Ranch, expanded to fifty-two hundred acres, was renamed Newhall Meridian Farms, and has become a showpiece of mechanized farming.

With that success in mind, company executives looked over the land at the New Columbia, where the black cattle grazed peacefully. Centuries of flooding by the sluggish San Joaquin River, followed by evaporation, had made the ground too salty for food crops. The fields had been planted only to barley and other grains that needed no irrigation. This kind of planting did little to stay erosion and nothing to conserve water. If the land could be properly leveled and graded for irrigation, and the alkali removed, both land and water would be put to better use. It was believed that most of the alkali could be removed by running water and by leaching the salts from the land below the root level. The insoluble black alkali could then be neutralized by adding chemicals. Field by field, the land at the New Columbia was improved. During the flooding stage, rice was sown by low-flying planes. When tests of the soil showed that it was salt-free, the land was planted with beets, barley, alfalfa, cotton, and corn. Adjoining lands were added to the original purchase until some 8,000 of 13,600 acres were brought under irrigation.

Since the New Columbia had proved more adaptable to farming than to cows, the hunt for a breeding ranch was resumed. In 1950 the company bought a spread of over one hundred thousand acres in Colorado, known as the Luis Maria Cabeza de Baca Grant, or, more generally, Baca Grant. Like the earliest Newhall ranches, it was a former Spanish grant. Located in the San Luis Valley, two hundred miles southwest of Denver, the Baca Grant contained artesian water in the meadows of the flat valley floor, and several streams poured through its boundaries from the four-teen-thousand-foot Sangre de Cristo Peaks that marked the ranch's limits. Unfortunately, the ranch was acquired early in the driest weather cycle in the history of the Southwest. The drought, plus the distance from the other ranches, has caused the directors to wonder again whether or not to stay in the breeding business.

Year-end inventories in the mid-1950's showed more than twenty thousand head of cattle on the various ranches. Of this total about one-quarter was in the breeding herd at the Baca Grant, another quarter in the feed pens at the Newhall Ranch, and the remaining half on the ranges. Cattle were still big business for The Newhall Land and Farming Company.

But farming, too, was big business. Success at the Newhall Meridian Farms and on the New Columbia had been demonstrated, and a great deal of heavy equipment had been acquired. One of the first occasions for using the equipment was in connection with the restoration of the flood-damaged land at the Newhall Ranch. In areas where the sand was excessively deep, it was removed in giant trucks, and where it lay to a depth of three feet or less, it was plowed under. Further use for the big equipment was found in leveling and draining the Meridian and New Columbia farmland.

As work at the New Columbia neared completion, another property, forty miles from the New Columbia, was offered for sale. Formerly part of the Miller & Lux grazing empire, the property contained 13,400 acres of rough land, some of which was alkaline. The company acquired the property and named it the Merced Ranch. In the first year of ownership the Newhall company prepared and planted two thousand acres. One of the beets grown in a new field weighed over thirty-four pounds and won a trip to Honolulu for the superintendent of the Merced Ranch.

The new company properties that were bought as cattle ranches and farmed only to grain and pasture have been developed for greater production. What was once wasted water now falls as man-made rain from extensive irrigation systems, and the new crops hold the land against the forces of erosion. In this land-improvement program, mechanization has played an important part. On the Meridian Ranch the plowing, sowing, thinning, and harvesting of sugar beets is mechanical. Four men and two machines now do the harvesting work that once required two hundred men. Investment in this specialized equipment yields more when spread over many acres, and the acreage has been mounting.

Along with cattle and farming, orchard development has continued at the Newhall Ranch. By the mid-thirties the original one hundred and fifty acres, planted in 1913, had increased to over three hundred acres of oranges. Little by little new fields were developed, hillsides were terraced to plant additional trees, and the acreage was again doubled. Today the valley at the western end of the ranch, adjoining Camulos, is covered with the solid dark green of orange trees. The varieties are both Valencias and navels.

The latest development in the navel grove extends back into Newhall family history. Almer Ives Hall, who hired Henry Mayo Newhall as an auctioneer in 1850, went back to Wallingford, Connecticut, where he married and joined his father's silver business. His wife having died when his children were small, it was his custom to bring them West on his business trips. His daughter Fannie was twenty-one when she married Henry Mayo Newhall's son Edwin. Five years after Fannie's tragic death in childbirth, Almer Hall lost his only son. Bereaved and in ill health, he decided to buy a small acreage in Duarte, east of Los Angeles, and raise oranges. He borrowed money from Walter Newhall to buy the ranch and lived there about five years until his death in 1897.

When Walter Newhall thus came into possession of forty acres in Duarte, he hired Billy Hagen, a German who had once been a coachman for his brother Henry, to manage the property. Either the soil was ideal or Billy Hagen had a way with oranges, for the small orchard produced excellent crops. When Walter died in 1906, the Duarte orchard was part of the trust held for his nieces and nephews. It was eventually sold after Billy Hagen died in the mid-thirties.

During Billy Hagen's tenure, Paul Hackney, Newhall orchard superintendent, looked over the Duarte. He noticed a single limb of one navel orange tree had fruit of an unusually deep orange color. Tests at the University of California experiment station showed that the deep-colored oranges from this tree had an exceptionally high sugar content. Buds were taken from the limb and grafted onto a tree at the Newhall orchard. The process of grafting was continued, and in 1950 Hackney had enough buds to graft forty-one trees. By 1956 there were nearly nine hundred trees bearing what are known as "Newhall Navels," and an additional twenty-one hundred trees, already budded, will be yielding in coming years the deep-colored sweet oranges of the Duarte limb.

In 1948 the management decided that many of the small fields that were too cold for oranges might be used for walnut planting. Young walnut trees were laid out in a narrow one-hundred-acre field along the Castaic-Ventura highway, and each year additional hilly land has been cleared and planted. A dehydrating plant, in which the walnuts have their hulls removed and are prepared for market, was built in 1952. By the end of 1955 there were 385 acres in walnuts.

The extension of the orchards brought up the question of water and the old agreement with the Del Valles at Camulos. As trees grew in number, The Newhall Land and Farming Company decided to build a pipe line to the orchards from Castaic Creek. However, the taking of water into a pipe line would change the flow of the Santa Clara River. Back in the 1880's, when the ranch borders between the Newhall land and Camulos were adjusted, it had been agreed to allow the Del Valles to dig a ditch to the river and take up to half the river water. The agreement, made formal in 1908, was filed in Ventura County in 1912. In 1924, with the third generation of Del Valles gone and prices in a post-war slump, the Del Valles sold Camulos. The next owner, August A. Rubel, continued to develop the orange groves. Rubel wanted to know what would happen to his grove if the Newhall company took the water in Castaic Creek and reduced the Santa Clara River to a trickle. In July 1938 Rubel and the Newhall company had failed to reach a settlement and Rubel filed suit. However, before the suit came to court, both parties assented to a new agreement. By its terms Rubel paid the cost of sufficiently enlarging the new pipe line to carry water for Camulos as well as for the Newhall orchards.

XV...*From Rancho to City*

THE NEWHALL LAND and Farming Company, once the property of one man, is now owned, in varying proportions, principally by that man's descendants. Henry Mayo Newhall today has fifty-four living descendants. If the husbands, wives, and stepchildren in the family are counted, there are approximately eighty people who share the family proprietary interest in the company's affairs. To that basic family ownership has recently been added a group of company executives. A stock-purchase plan has been developed to allow the men who have participated in the operation of the company to share in its ownership.

On the fourteen-man board of directors are eight descendants of H. M. Newhall, four San Francisco business leaders who are not connected with the family, and the president and operating head, George E. Bushell. The chairman of the board, Atholl Mc-Bean, is a family member by marriage. It is a far cry from the easygoing days when five brothers sat down informally in meeting, as well as from the depression time when only one Newhall sat on a seven-man board. Since those days another generation has come of age. There are now five of H. M. Newhall's great-grandsons on the board. In addition two family members are among the company's three hundred employees: Peter McBean, a grandson of Mayo, and Edwin Newhall Woods, grandson of Edwin Newhall. Bushell became president in 1950 when Atholl McBean stepped into the newly created position of chairman of the board. The company has been thoroughly departmentalized, and no longer are company executives appointed because they are Newhalls or know how to handle a lasso. They are, by and large, graduates of leading universities in technical fields.

Ranch employees are skilled workmen. They share in company-supported programs of life, health, accident, and retirement insurance and are active participants in schools, churches, 4-H Clubs, and other community activities in the ranch areas. Some are of the second generation; for instance, the superintendent of the New Columbia Ranch, an employee's son, grew up on the Newhall Meridian Farms. In 1945 a sum of $30,000 and fifteen acres of land were contributed to the town of Newhall for the H. M. Newhall Memorial Swimming Pool and Recreation Center, which was dedicated in 1949.

It was in 1886 that Henry G. Newhall, president of The Newhall Land and Farming Company, formed three years earlier, suggested that the land on the Rancho San Francisco be surveyed, water resources estimated, roads laid out, and a water company formed. Seventy years later his program is being carried out. A Development Department was created in 1954. Three restaurants, service stations, and other small business enterprises have been built by the company and leased successfully. A water company has been formed for more efficient handling of the company's water resources; state and county highway engineers are being consulted in mapping roads through the ranch.

The executive offices of The Newhall Land and Farming Company are at Castaic Junction, where United States Highway 99, the main artery of travel between San Francisco and Los Angeles, meets the highway to Ventura. Don Gaspar de Portolá described the spot as "a place called Castec," where once five Indian villages were centered. A few hundred yards away is the site of Antonio del Valle's adobe house, and here is where Henry Newhall pitched his tents to "go warring with the powers of Nature."

Atholl McBean, Chairman of the Board of The Newhall Land and Farming Company.

The country around this spot is still pastoral, though the flatland is covered with field crops and an occasional oil rig interrupts the vista of rugged hills. People of the Newhall company know, with some regret, that their peaceful acres will not long lie undisturbed. A rising tide of people has overflowed the Los Angeles basin—especially the San Fernando Valley—and spilled out over the hills on all sides. State plans provide for a freeway, soon to be built, linking the ranch to the city, which will place the ranch lands a mere forty minutes from the center of Los Angeles.

If the city dwellers come to establish houses, schools, and factories on the Newhall Ranch, it will be nothing more than Henry Mayo Newhall expected. He lived and made his fortune furthering growth and development. The ranches today, and the outlook for the future, stand as a testimonial to the vision of a man who could see over the hills and into the fertile valleys beyond.

Appendix

THE WILL OF
HENRY MAYO NEWHALL

I, Henry Mayo Newhall,

1. Will and direct that my Executrix and Executors shall pay all my just debts, etc., out of the proceeds of my personal property and out of the income, profits, and revenue of real estate, not resorting to the sale of real estate for that purpose unless in their judgment it is absolutely necessary.

2. Give, devise, and bequeath to my wife Margaret J. Newhall, during her life my present homestead lot, appurtenances, etc., and stable lot and lots adjoining, etc., in San Francisco on the southwest corner of Sutter street and Van Ness avenue extending back to the north line of Post street on the south, or any other or new homestead I may have and occupy at the time of my decease, together with all household furniture thereon and all goods, personal property, etc. used in and about said homestead and premises, for a home for my wife and five sons; said homestead, furniture, etc., with all my watches and jewelry, carriages, horses, etc. to be held and used by my wife during her life and on her decease to pass to my executors and survivor and survivors of them and heirs of survivor in trust for use and behoof of my five sons, Henry Gregory Newhall, William Mayo Newhall, Edwin White Newhall, Walter Scott Newhall, and George Almer Newhall, to which executors and survivors, etc. I give and bequeath said homestead or other substituted homestead etc. in fee simple in trust for only use and behoof of said five children share and share alike, subject to the foregoing interest given to my wife during her life. And executors shall convey and deliver same in full property and ownership to said five children share and share alike at a time and in a manner and under circumstances hereinafter set forth.

3. Give and bequeath to Margery Palache, wife of Gilbert Palache, $10,000 to and for her separate use, as, and for her separate property, and estate: Also, give and bequeath to Sarah Ann Newhall Palache and Ida Palache $10,000 each to remain as their

own separate property and estate absolutely, and further, give and bequeath to Gilbert Palache in trust for his son Thomas Hood Palache $1000 to be invested and reinvested by Gilbert Palache and his successor and successors in trust for Thomas Hood Palache until he attain age of 21 years at which time principal and interest shall be paid to him absolutely, or earlier in case of absolute necessity to be determined by Trustee: in case of the death of said Thomas before majority, Trustee shall pay principal and interest, or so much as there may be, to executors for use etc. of my five sons share and share alike, if my youngest son be then of age to be paid to them absolutely, etc.

4. All real estate of which I may die seized and possessed, or in which I have any right, title, or interest, wherever situate, and all moneys, personal property, assets and effects of every kind and nature except such as is herein devised and bequeathed to other persons, I give, devise, and bequeath to my Executrix and Executors, that is to such of them as shall accept the trust and to the survivors and survivor of them in trust, to and for uses and purposes following:

As speedily as practicable after my death, Executrix and Executors shall reduce all of my personal assets and effects, except household furniture, personal property, jewelry, etc., as shall be at my homestead or used about same, at my decease, into money, and after payment of my debts, etc., and specific legacies and gifts herein directed to be paid out of same, Executrix and Executors shall invest said money with that on hand at the time of my death and that thereafter collected without sales of real estate for use and benefit of my five sons, share and share alike, to be transferred and delivered to them at the time and in the manner hereinafter set forth, or Executrix and Executors may at their option use and employ said moneys or any part thereof from time to time in improvement of real estate of which I may die seized or which Executrix and Executors may purchase out of proceeds of personal effects and assets, and income and revenue of all real estate mentioned and referred to in this section shall be used and applied as herein below directed.

I further will and direct that when my youngest son, George Almer Newhall, shall attain the age of 21 years, and not before,

Executrix and Executors shall convey transfer and assign over fully and absolutely in fee simple and ownership to my five sons as tenants in common share and share alike all said real estate and all assets of every kind and character remaining in their hands, with the increase, income, profits, and accumulations thereof in whatever form consisting, all of which I hereby give, devise, and bequeath to my five sons share and share alike at the time and in the manner aforesaid: and in case of the death of my wife during the minority of my youngest son, the share herein given to my wife in the homestead etc. shall pass to my five children share and share alike in like manner as above provided for their interests and in like manner held in trust and used by executors for them until my youngest son attain majority, at which time same shall be conveyed and delivered by my five sons share and share alike in the same manner and time that other property bequeathed to them is to be conveyed and delivered to them; provided that if my wife shall still survive when my youngest son shall attain his majority, then my homestead or any homestead I may leave at my death, with all personal property thereabouts, shall still remain for use and benefit of my wife until her death; and executors, out of funds of estate in their hands shall at all times during the life of my wife pay to her and for her own use and to and for such purposes as she may see fit to apply the same, any and all money from time to time as she may require and request of them to pay to her and her receipt therefor shall be full release and discharge to them therefor.

5. Will, and earnestly enjoin Executors and especially my wife to see that my children are respectably reared, supported, and maintained, that their morals, health, and education receive the greatest care and attention, and enjoin upon my children to treat and regard my wife with utmost affection and protect and comfort her.

6. If any of my children die before my decease, the share of such deceased child or children shall pass to my other children in the same manner, time, and form as same would have passed to dec'd had he, or they, survived. So, also upon death of any of my children under the age of 21 years, share of dec'd child or children shall pass to surviving children in the same manner,

form, and time as it would have passed to dec'd had he or they survived. Should my wife not be living at my decease, all gifts, bequests, legacies, annuities herein, given to her, shall pass to surviving executors in trust for use and benefit of my children in the same manner, time, and form as above in reference to other gifts, devises, and bequests for use and benefit of my children.

7. All legacies, annuities, gifts, and bequests herein made to any person who shall not be living at the time of my decease shall lapse, cease, and be taken with the bulk of my estate in trust for my wife and children as if expressly included in the parts herein above given for use and benefit of my wife and children.

8. Hereby nominate and appoint my wife, Margaret Jane Newhall, and sons Henry G. Newhall and William M. Newhall and friend Gilbert Palache, and survivor and survivors of them to be Executrix and Executors of this will, and as such trustee of the various trusts herein created, also guardians of my minor children: on any difference of opinion or judgment in said matters within their discretion, I authorize and empower the majority of them to decide and determine. No bond or other security shall be required from any or either as executrix, executors, trustees, or guardians at any time. On failure of either or inability to accept said offices and trusts, the powers, rights, interests, estate, and trusts given to and invested in all shall pass to, and be vested in, such as do accept said offices and trusts, and in the survivors and survivor of them. And I direct Executrix and Executors to select for legal adviser, counsel, and Attorney Samuel M. Wilson, or Russell J. Wilson, in case of his death.

I declare this to be my last will, revoking all former wills, etc.

June 23, 1880

Executed etc. in the presence of and attested by
William Alvord
Thomas Brown
Russell J. Wilson
all of San Francisco.

Recorded April 11, 1882
San Francisco

TRANSLATION OF THE WILL OF
IGNACIO DEL VALLE

In the name of Almighty God, I, Ignacio del Valle, a native of the City of Compostela in the Republic of Mexico, sixty-one years of age, legitimate son of D. Antonio Seferino del Valle and Da. Maria Josefa de la Peña, finding myself through Divine Providence well and in the possession of all my faculties, believing and acknowledging as I firmly believe and acknowledge the mystery of the Holy Trinity and the redemption of man by the death of our Lord Jesus Christ, and all the other mysteries and sacraments which our Holy Mother the Roman Catholic Apostolic Church believes and acknowledges, in which true faith and belief I live and hope to die; and fearing the death which is so natural and inevitable to all human creatures and so uncertain the hour, I declare, make, order, and publish my last will in the following form: I commend my Soul to God our Lord, who created it from nothing and consign my body to the earth whence it was formed.

1st. After paying all my just debts I give and bequeath to my beloved wife Isabel and to my legitimate children born prior to the time of my death and those born subsequently of my said wife Isabel conceived by her of me, all of my property, real and personal, in the proportions of one-third part to my said wife and two-third parts to our children had of our marriage; which two-third parts bequeathed to our children shall be fairly distributed to them in equal shares in value, without the intervention of Probate or any other Court.

2nd. I give and bequeath to my said wife Isabel del Valle the sole and entire management of all my property, real and personal, during the term of her life or until she marries again, for the benefit of herself and the children had between us, free from the intervention and direction of any Probate or any other Court or Courts of this or any other State; it being my will that all my property remain undivided until the death of my aforesaid wife or until she marries again, unless she should decide to make a partition of my property before that time in which case she may and by this document has authority to divide it, being responsible for her acts only to God and her own conscience.

3rd. I bequeath and give to my aforesaid wife Isabel full and complete power during her performance of the duties of executrix of this my last will and testament, to sell, transfer, or exchange in her own name any portion or all of my real or personal property and to give deed for the same. She is likewise authorized to buy other property in case she believes it to be advantageous to her own interests and those of our children had between us without the intervention of any Court.

4th. By this my last will I appoint my aforesaid wife Isabel guardian of all our children had between us, of the persons of our said children as well as of the property belonging to them, while she may consider it advisable in her judgment to hold possession of the interests of all or some of our said children for their benefit. Consequently I exempt her from giving any bonds as well as from rendering any account of her administration to the Probate or any other Court as the guardian appointed by me by this my last will.

5th. I appoint as my executors in the first place my dear wife Isabel and in the second place my best friend and *compadre* D. Ulpiano Indart and exempt them both from giving any bond as my executors.

6th. In case that my aforesaid wife should marry again or in case of her death during the minority of our aforesaid children, in either of these cases I appoint by this my last will my friend D. Ulpiano Indart guardian of the persons and estate of my children engendered in the body of my aforesaid wife Isabel and hereby authorize my said friend D. Ulpiano Indart to take immediate possession of the property belonging to my aforesaid children, who are not of legal age, and in such case I request him to make an inventory of the property that he takes in his possession and to deposit the same in the Probate Court of the County of his residence; it being well understood that he is by these presents relieved from giving any bonds or security whatever as such guardian, for the reason that I have full confidence in his honesty and integrity and because of this I give him full power to sell any personal property belonging to my children privately or in the manner that he deems more advantageous to the interests of my said children. In testimony whereof I sign these presents at the Rancho of Camulos, state of California, County of Santa Barbara, and I affix my seal this the first day of January 1870.

[Signed] Ignacio del Valle

Ignacio del Valle having signed the foregoing document in the presence of each one of us, said Ignacio del Valle declared to us that it was his last will and testament and he requested us to sign as witnesses to having seen him sign it on the date written in the will and we in his presence and in the presence of each other at the request of the testator wrote our names as witnesses of the date, but not of the will this first day of January 1870.

C. A. Thompson
S. F. Cooper
J. M. Horton
José Ignacio del Valle
Anastacio Rubio

Endorsed

Filed for Probate this 29th day of April 1880.

L. F. Eastin, Clerk.

In the Superior Court in and for the County of
  Ventura, State of California

In the matter of the estate of   Letters Testamentary
Ignacio del Valle   Deceased

Index